DATE DUE

Meaning in Life
and Why It Matters

The University Center for Human Values Series

Charles R. Beitz, Editor

Multiculturalism and "The Politics of Recognition"
by Charles Taylor

A Matter of Interpretation: Federal Courts and the Law
by Antonin Scalia

Freedom of Association edited by Amy Gutmann

Work and Welfare by Robert M. Solow

The Lives of Animals by J. M. Coetzee

Truth v. Justice: The Morality of Truth Commissions
edited by Robert I. Rotberg and Dennis Thompson

Goodness and Advice by Judith Jarvis Thomson

Human Rights as Politics and Idolatry
by Michael Ignatieff

Democracy, Culture, and the Voice of Poetry
by Robert Pinsky

Primates and Philosophers: How Morality Evolved
by Frans de Waal

*Striking First: Preemption and Prevention
in International Conflict*
by Michael W. Doyle

Meaning in Life and Why It Matters by Susan Wolf

The Limits of Constitutional Democracy
edited by Jeffrey K. Tulis and Stephen Macedo

Meaning in Life
and Why It Matters

Susan Wolf

Introduction by
Stephen Macedo

With Commentary by
John Koelhe, Robert M. Adams,
Nomy Arpaly, and Jonathan Haidt

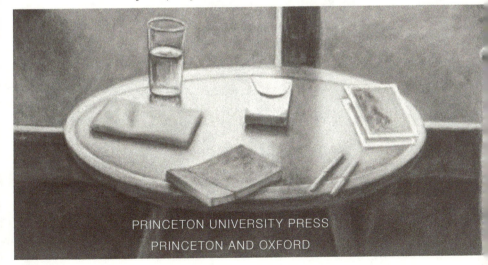

PRINCETON UNIVERSITY PRESS

PRINCETON AND OXFORD

Copyright © 2010 by Princeton University Press
Published by Princeton University Press, 41 William Street,
Princeton, New Jersey 08540
In the United Kingdom: Princeton University Press, 6 Oxford Street,
Woodstock, Oxfordshire OX20 1TW

press.princeton.edu

Third printing, and first paperback printing, 2012
Paperback ISBN 978-0-691-15450-3

The Library of Congress has cataloged the cloth edition
of this book as follows

Wolf, Susan R.
Meaning in life and why it matters / Susan Wolf ; introduction by
Stephen Macedo ; with commentary by John Koethe . . . [et al.].
p. cm. — (The University Center for Human Values series)
These essays were formerly lectures delivered at
Princeton University in Nov. 2007.
Includes bibliographical references and index.
ISBN 978-0-691-14524-2 (hardback : alk. paper)
1. Life. 2. Values. I. Koethe, John, 1945– II. Title.
BD431.W77 2010
170—dc22
2009036206

British Library Cataloging-in-Publication Data is available

This book has been composed in Adobe Caslon Pro

Printed on acid-free paper. ∞

Printed in the United States of America

Book design by Marcella Engel Roberts

3 5 7 9 10 8 6 4

For Katie and Lisa

Contents

Acknowledgments

I HAVE BEEN THINKING, talking, and writing about topics related to these lectures for many years and have benefited from discussions with more friends, colleagues, and students than I can mention. In addition to the Tanner Foundation and Princeton University, though, I owe special debts of gratitude to several institutions, which I would like to acknowledge here. The Guggenheim Foundation and the Australian National University sponsored a year of research in which I began developing my ideas on meaningfulness. The Mellon Foundation sponsored a second trip to the ANU as well as providing resources that have made my last few years of teaching and research especially pleasant and rewarding. Finally, I thank the University of North Carolina at Chapel Hill and especially the philosophy department, for providing as stimulating and supportive an academic community as anyone could wish for.

Susan Wolf
July 21, 2009

Introduction

Stephen Macedo

SUSAN WOLF'S TOPIC in these essays—formerly lectures delivered at Princeton University in November 2007—is familiar and inescapable, and yet the topic has not received sustained philosophical attention. Her subject is not the question of the ultimate meaning of human life: whether humans are part of a larger narrative or higher purpose or plan of the sort associated with religious traditions. Nor does Wolf make it her project to fend off existential dread or the fear that, absent some larger narrative, human life must ultimately be meaningless, snuffed out by death and the eventual implosion of the universe. Nor, finally, do these lectures propound a particular recipe for constructing a meaningful life, though Wolf does help clarify what it means to do so and why it matters.

We all seek meaning in our lives and recognize meaning's absence in lives characterized by boredom, dullness, alienation, and listless disengagement. But what is meaning in life? Is it distinctive, or reducible to other aims and conceptions? Is it a helpful category for thinking about good lives that are worth living? Is it sensible and coherent to want it in one's life?

Wolf seeks to explicate, defend, and secure the category of meaningfulness as a distinctive dimension of good lives. She distinguishes it from two other categories; namely, happiness, often associated with rational egoism, and morality, often associated with an impartial concern with human well-being. Meaningfulness is neither of these, on Wolf's view, but it is much to be sought for and an essential element of a fully satisfying life.

Wolf argues in her first lecture that meaning in life is best understood in terms of Fitting Fulfillment. According to her, "meaning in life arises when subjective attraction meets objective attractiveness, and one is able to do something about it or with it." The three crucial elements are subjective attraction, objective worthiness, and active, productive engagement. Human beings long for fulfillment, on Wolf's view, and we admire people whose lives are lovingly and productively engaged with projects that are worthy of engagement.

But exactly how should we understand the different elements of meaningful lives? Are all of them necessary? Are there aspects of meaningfulness that Wolf has not identified? Is Wolf right to insist on the importance of objective standards of worth or fittingness: to claim that we ought to engage with something larger than ourselves or at least something outside of ourselves? Does she risk being too judgmental, or even elitist? Or, rather, is she not judgmental enough?

Wolf pursues her inquiry with rigor and subtlety, in part via an "endoxic method" that takes seriously what ordinary people say about their desire for meaning in their lives. The view she develops supports what ordinary people often say about the importance of living meaningful lives, and so, Wolf's account helps vindicate much human striving. The essays that follow, including the commentaries, do not rest on abstractions alone but are richly illustrated with both hypothetical and real cases. This is philosophy at its best: grappling clear-mindedly with a familiar category of value whose import and structure are nevertheless far from clear and whose reality might even be doubted. Wolf makes a powerful case that *meaning in life* does amount to an essential evaluative standard for human well-being.

Wolf's two essays on meaning in life are followed by four critical but constructive commentaries. John Koethe and Robert Adams are largely sympathetic to Wolf's project, and seek to clarify the subjective and objective elements of meaning in life. Nomy Arpaly and Jonathan Haidt express some skepticism about parts of Wolf's account, and question the need for criteria of objective value.

John Koethe—philosopher and poet—interrogates Wolf's account of meaning in life from the point of view of artistic endeavor, including painting and poetry, and especially the avant-garde. Here, judgments about whether projects are ultimately worthwhile and contribute to meaning seem especially controversial and uncertain, in part because the criteria for success and their application—*You call that art?*—are so often contested and contestable. When Wolf calls a project or activity objectively valuable, does she mean that it is of a *kind* we value, or, that in this case the project or activity has been successfully pursued? In some fields—engineering for example—there would seem to be straightforward tests of success (did the building survive the earthquake?). But the dividing line between successful, meaningful artistic endeavor and failed or bogus attempts is vague and contested, especially for innovators. And yet the question of success matters to our assessment of lives. If Gauguin can be excused for neglecting his family to pursue his calling as an artist, this is so at least partly because his art turned out to be a magnificent success. But what if he were an "untalented hack"? When and how can we know for sure? Koethe argues that with respect to many aesthetic endeavors, "the possibility of delusion is internal to them," and the line between greatness and fraudulence is often fine and shifting.

If Koethe focuses on the objective dimension of worthiness, Robert Adams takes up the subjective dimension of fulfillment, wondering whether and in what sense "fulfill-ment" is crucial to meaningfulness in life. He doubts that *feelings* of fulfillment are essential to the meaningful life. Ful-fillment, in the sense of *actual success* in one's projects, may matter more. Great success surely contributes to meaning-fulness, but is at least some modicum of success essential if a life is to be regarded as meaningful? Adams argues that in fact a magnificent but failed project might make for a highly meaningful life, and he offers as an example the mastermind of the failed plot to kill Hitler in the waning months of World War II.

Adams further considers some suggestive analogies be-tween meaning in life and other sorts of meaning, including in the use of language. Finally, he explores the relationship between the objective dimensions of meaning in life and im-partial morality, suggesting that these may be more closely and completely related than Wolf suggests. What should we think about those who oppose evil, but do so based not on impartial moral considerations, but rather out of patriotism or love of country or some other partial motive? Must im-partial moral judgment be brought to bear to insure that love takes its proper—or at least a morally acceptable—object?

Nomy Arpaly questions the role that Wolf claims for "ob-jective worth" in providing meaning in life. It is enough to say of a life that it was fulfilling for the person who lived it, she argues, without having to add that it was fit for fulfill-ment according to some objective criteria. If we are lucky enough to spend our lives engaged with the things we care most about, why isn't that sufficient? Why add that there must be a modicum of objective worth? After all, says Arpaly, no normal adult would be fulfilled by, say, a life spent gazing at a goldfish. Insofar as particular people claim to be fulfilled entirely by their relationship with their pets, they typically are mistaken about the facts (for example, exaggerating the cognitive capacity of cats and dogs by suggesting that "only my pet understands me"). Or, they may be people who lack certain human capacities, so that caring for a pet is in truth the limit of their capability. The mentally retarded really may be fulfilled in significant part by successfully keeping a pet. No appeal to objective value is needed here, Arpaly argues, only an appeal to intuitions and evidence about what in fact fulfills humans as we know them.

Arpaly raises the additional question of whether meaningfulness is itself properly understood as a reason for which we act. We act for the sake of the things we love and are devoted to, she insists, not for the sake of meaningfulness. To do things *because* they contribute to meaning in life is "one thought too many."

Jonathan Haidt argues that psychology helps illuminate two elements that are key to the achievement of meaningfulness in human life. One is the idea of vital engagement, which is characterized by experiences of "flow," defined as enjoyed absorption and deep interest in a project around which people build their lives and relationships. Meaningful, generative lives are characterized by vital engagement. Haidt argues that vital engagement does not need to be supplemented by any idea of objective value. Like Arpaly, Haidt argues that there is no danger that normal human beings will find fulfillment—or vital engagement—in lives dedicated to goldfish gazing, flagpole sitting, lawn mower racing, or other amusements that people sometimes engage in just for fun. A philosophical account of objective value is not only superfluous, Haidt suggests, but positively dangerous, since such an account could fall prey to elitism, wrongly ruling out activities that people do deeply and productively engage with, such as the care and breeding of horses.

Psychology's second crucial insight for understanding meaning in life, says Haidt, is hive psychology. Human beings are "ultrasocial," not individualistic, and in this we more closely resemble "bees, ants, termites, and naked mole rats" than our ancestors the chimpanzees. Meaningfulness would be more easily achieved, Haidt suggests, if we placed the group rather than the individual at the center of our thinking about fulfilled lives, and recognized the importance of participation in collective rituals and projects.

In her response to these friendly but perceptive critics, Wolf extends and deepens her argument, acknowledging ways in which the commentators help refine her basic view. She resists the suggestion that we would do well to dispense with objective judgments about worthiness or fittingness when thinking about the activities that contribute to meaning in life. Objective standards can help us understand why some activities are not properly objects of deep engagement and loving attention. Insofar as a belief in objective standards of fittingness leads us to question whether great attention should be lavished on horse breeding, analytic philosophy, or any number of other pursuits whose value might be doubted, that belief is a good thing. Wolf argues that we should welcome critical reflection on our success in discerning and pursuing projects that are both fulfilling and genuinely worthwhile.

These essays—philosophically rigorous but also accessible, topical, and colorfully written—do not purport to be the last words on these vital and inescapable questions. They are, however, a terrific place to begin thinking seriously about meaning in life and why it matters.

Princeton
July 2009

Meaning in Life and Why It Matters
Susan Wolf

Meaning in Life

A False Dichotomy

PHILOSOPHICAL MODELS of human psychology—or, more specifically, of human motivation—tend to fall into one of two categories. Perhaps the oldest and most popular model conceives of human beings as egoists, moved and guided exclusively by what they take to be in their own self-interest. However, there have long been defenders of a dualistic model of motivation as well, according to which people are capable of being moved not only by self-interest, but also by something "higher." Kant, for example, famously thought that in addition to being subject to inclinations, people are capable of being moved and directed by reason alone.

Closely linked to these two descriptive models of human motivation are prescriptive or normative models of practical reason. The descriptive thesis of psychological egoism, which holds that people exclusively seek their own good, is closely connected to (and frequently confused with) the normative thesis of rational egoism, which holds that people are only rational insofar as they seek to maximize their welfare. Corresponding to the dual conception of human motivation we find a dual conception of practical reason as well. This is perhaps most explicit in the writings of Henry Sidgwick, who held that two perspectives offer people equally valid reasons to act: the egoistic perspective, which issues recommendations of what is most in an agent's self-interest; and the impersonal perspective, which urges one to do what is best "from the point of view of the universe."

In ordinary discourse as well as philosophy we seem to have one of these two models in the backs of our minds when we offer justifications for our actions or our policies. Most often, when asked to explain or justify our choices, we offer reasons that seem to fall under the category of self-interest. When we are trying to persuade *someone else* to do something, we may appeal to self-interest—in this case, to the *other* person's self-interest—even more. Still, there are some occasions when invoking self-interest would simply be unconvincing, and others when such appeals would be unseemly, or at least beside the point. In these cases, we are likely to speak the language of duty: justice, compassion, or, simply, morality demands that we act in such and such a way, whether it contributes to our own good or not.

These models of motivation and practical reason, however, seem to me to leave out many of the motives and reasons that shape our lives. Moreover, the reasons left out are neither peripheral nor eccentric. Indeed, we might say that the reasons and motives omitted by these models are some of the most important and central ones in our lives. They are the reasons and motives that engage us in the activities that make our lives worth living; they give us a reason to go on; they make our worlds go round. They, and the activities they engender, give meaning to our lives.

My aim in this lecture is to bring out the distinctive character of these sorts of reasons and the special role they play in the quality of our lives. Specifically, I shall suggest that our susceptibility to these sorts of reasons is connected to the possibility that we live meaningful lives, understanding meaningfulness as an attribute lives can have that is not reducible to or subsumable under either happiness, as it is ordinarily understood, or morality. I shall be mainly concerned to explain the feature I call meaningfulness in life and to present it in such a way as to make it seem worth wanting, both for ourselves and for those about whom we care. As will be seen, however, what I have to say will be of little or no *practical* use. Though I shall offer a view of what it means for a life to be meaningful, I can offer only the most abstract advice about how to go about getting or living such a life. In my second lecture therefore, after defending my view against one particularly important set of objections, I shall turn to the question of why it matters that we notice that there is such a category as meaningfulness, distinct from the categories of happiness and morality that we are more used to invoking in thinking about what to do and how to live. As I shall argue, awareness that meaning is a third sort of value a life can possess should affect our understanding of the first two sorts: that is, adopting models of human motivation and reason that are attentive to meaningfulness should affect the way we think about happiness and morality—and about self-interest as well. Moreover, if the view I present in these lectures is right, we cannot so much as conceive of meaning without attributing a certain sort of objectivity to value judgments. It follows that if we want to continue to talk about, attend to, and encourage the acquisition of meaning in people's lives, we need to be willing to admit this sort of objectivity into our discussion of values.

Let me begin with some examples of the sorts of reasons and motives I have in mind—reasons and motives that are not best understood in terms of their contributions to either our happiness or our sense of what impersonal reason or morality demands. The most obvious examples of what I have in mind occur when we act out of love for individuals about whom we deeply and especially care. When I visit my brother in the hospital, or help my friend move, or stay up all night sewing my daughter a Halloween costume, I act neither for egoistic reasons nor for moral ones. I do not believe that it is better *for me* that I spend a depressing hour in a drab, cramped room, seeing my brother irritable and in pain, that I risk back injury trying to get my friend's sofa safely down two flights of stairs, or that I forego hours of much-wanted sleep to make sure that the wings will stand out at a good angle from the butterfly costume my daughter wants to wear in the next day's parade. But neither do I believe myself duty-bound to perform these acts, or fool myself into thinking that by doing them I do what will be best for the world. I act neither out of self-interest nor out of duty or any other sort of impersonal or impartial reason. Rather, I act out of love.

As the egoistic and dualist models of practical reason leave out what we might call these "reasons of love,"[1] so they seem to me also to leave out many of the reasons that move us to pursue nonpersonal interests about which we are especially passionate. Writing philosophy, practicing the cello, keeping one's garden free of weeds, may demand more of one's time and attention than would be optimal from the point of view of one's own well-being. Yet in these cases, even more than in the cases involving beloved human beings, it is obvious that no impersonal perspective requires us to act. Just as, in

---

[1] The phrase is used by Harry Frankfurt in much the same way as I use it and for purposes that largely overlap with mine in Harry Frankfurt, *The Reasons of Love* (Princeton: Princeton University Press, 2004). Like me, Frankfurt sees our susceptibility to reasons of love as essential to the possibility that we live meaningful lives. He forcefully rejects the conditions on which reasons for love can ground claims of meaning that I defend in what follows, however.

the case of acting for a loved one, it is the good of that other person that provides us with a reason for our action, what draws us on in the nonpersonal pursuits I have in mind is a perceived or imagined value that lies outside of oneself. I agonize over the article I am trying to write because I want to get it right—that is, because I want the argument to be sound, the view to be correct, the writing to be clear and graceful. It is not for my sake—at least not only for my sake—that I struggle so with my work. I do not know or care whether it is best for me—that is, whether it is best from the point of view of my self-interest—that I try to improve my work beyond a certain point, any more than I care whether it is best for me that I put so much energy into making my daughter happy. We might say that I struggle "for philosophy's sake" rather than for my own, but that would be misleading and obscure as well as pretentious. Still, it seems to me that it is the value of good philosophy that is driving and guiding my behavior in this instance, as it might be the beauty of the music or of the potential garden that moves the cellist or gardener to sacrifice ease and exercise discipline in pursuing her goal.

It does not seem unnatural or forced to speak of the subjects of these examples as *loving* philosophy or music or flowers, and their love for these things may not only explain but may also justify (or, more strictly, may contribute to the justification of) their choices and behavior more than their love for themselves or for morality or for some other impersonal and general good. Because of the similarities in the motivational and deliberative stance of these subjects to that of people who act out of love for individuals, I shall use the phrase "reasons of love" to cover both types of cases. My claim then is that reasons of love—whether of human individuals, other living creatures, or activities, ideals or objects of other sorts—have a distinctive and important role in our lives. They are not to be assimilated to reasons of self-interest or reasons of morality. Insofar as we fail to recognize and appreciate the legitimacy and value of these reasons, we misunderstand our values and ourselves and distort our concerns.

Not all actions that are motivated and guided by reasons of love are justified, however. Not all reasons of love are good reasons. For one thing, your love for something or someone is no guarantee that you know what is actually good for them. You may mean to help the object of your love, but your action may not benefit it. You might spoil your child, overwater your plants, cramp your philosophical style.

More interestingly, love can be misplaced or misguided; the energy or attention that you give to an object of love may be disproportionate to what that object merits.[2] A wonderful woman might give up her career, her home, her friendships to follow and serve a man the rest of us see does not "deserve her." An impressionable teenager might sign over his trust fund to a cult with which he has become enamored, thereby losing both his financial security and the opportunity to benefit worthier and needier groups.

What I wish to defend, then, is the justifiability and importance of a subset of those actions and decisions that are guided by reasons of love. Roughly, I want to defend the claim that acting in a way that positively engages with a *worthy* object of love can be perfectly justified even if it does not

---

[2] The first way in which reasons of love may be mistaken parallels mistakes to which what we might call "reasons of self-interest" and "reasons of morality" are subject. I may think that something is in my self-interest when it is actually harmful; I may think morality requires or allows me to do what in fact is morally wrong. It is not obvious that the second way in which an apparent reason of love can be wrong has parallels in these other categories. There may be no such thing as caring too much about one's own good or about morality.

maximally promote either the agent's welfare or the good of the world, impartially assessed.

Actions and decisions based on the good of the beloved are part and parcel of love and its expression quite generally. When, in addition, the object of love is specified to be worthy of love, the justification of action on behalf of that object may be straightforward. Why shouldn't it be as justifiable for a person to act on behalf of a friend, for example, as it is for her to act on her own behalf? And why shouldn't it be as justifiable to act on behalf of one's friend as it is to do something of greater benefit to the world at large? Unless rational egoism or a particularly extreme form of consequentialism is presupposed, there is no reason to doubt the rational permissibility of acting on such reasons of love. Still, I want to say something stronger, something more favorable and more supportive of reasons of this sort. More precisely, I want to say something more favorable about a life that is prone to being moved and guided by such reasons. Proneness to being moved and guided by such reasons, I believe, is at the core of our ability to live meaningful lives. But it is far from clear what saying this amounts to.

A Conception of Meaningfulness in Life

Academic philosophers do not talk much about meaningfulness in life. The term is more likely to be used by theologians or therapists, and by people who are in some way dissatisfied with their lives but are unable to pin down why. People sometimes complain that their lives lack meaning; they yearn for meaning; they seek meaning. People sometimes judge others to be leading exceptionally meaningful lives, looking upon them with envy or admiration. Meaning is commonly associated with a kind of depth. Often the need for meaning is connected to the sense that one's life is empty or shallow. An interest in meaning is also frequently associated with thoughts one might have on one's deathbed, or in contemplation of one's eventual death. When the word "meaningful" is used in characterizing a life (or in characterizing what is missing from a life), it calls *something* to mind, but it is not clear what, nor is it clear that it calls or is meant to call the same thing to mind in all contexts.

In offering a conception of meaningfulness, I do not wish to insist that the term is always used in the same way, or that what I have to offer as an analysis of meaningfulness can be substituted for that term in every context. On the other hand, I do believe that much talk of meaning is aimed at capturing the same abstract idea, and that my proposal of what that idea is fits well with many of the uses to which the word is put. Whether or not my idea of meaningfulness captures what others mean when they use the term, it is an idea of philosophical interest, for it is an idea of a significant way in which a life can be good, a category or dimension of value, if you will, which we have a serious reason to want for ourselves and for those we care about, and which is neither subsumable under nor reducible to either happiness or morality.

According to the conception of meaningfulness I wish to propose, meaning arises from loving objects worthy of love and engaging with them in a positive way. The words "love" and "objects," however, are in some ways misleadingly specific, "engaging [with objects] in a positive way" regrettably vague, and the description of some objects but not others as being "*worthy* of love" may be thought to be contentious. Rather than try to clarify the view by taking up one word or phrase at a time, let me try to describe the view in other terms, bringing out what I take to be salient.

What is perhaps most distinctive about my conception of meaning, or about the category of value I have in mind, is that it involves subjective and objective elements, suitably and inextricably linked. "Love" is at least partly subjective, involving attitudes and feelings. In insisting that the requisite object must be "worthy of love," however, this conception of meaning invokes an objective standard. It is implicit in insisting that an object be worthy of love (in order to contribute meaning to the lover's life) that not any object will do. Nor is it guaranteed that the subject's own assessment of worthiness is privileged. One might paraphrase this by saying that, according to my conception, meaning arises when subjective attraction meets objective attractiveness.

Essentially, the idea is that a person's life can be meaningful only if she cares fairly deeply about some thing or things, only if she is gripped, excited, interested, engaged, or as I earlier put it, if she loves something—as opposed to being bored by or alienated from most or all that she does. Even a person who is so engaged, however, will not live a meaningful life if the objects or activities with which she is so occupied are worthless. A person who loves smoking pot all day long, or doing endless crossword puzzles, and has the luxury of being able to indulge in this without restraint does not thereby make her life meaningful. Finally, this conception of meaning specifies that the relationship between the subject and the object of her attraction must be an active one. The condition that says that meaning involves engaging with the (worthy) object of love in a positive way is meant to make clear that mere passive recognition and a positive attitude toward an object's or activity's value is not sufficient for a meaningful life. One must be able to be in some sort of relationship with the valuable object of one's attention—to create it, protect it, promote it, honor it, or more generally, to actively affirm it in some way or other.

Aristotle is well known for his use of the endoxic method in defending moral and conceptual claims. That is, he takes the *endoxa*,[3] "the things which are accepted by everyone, or by most people or by the wise" as a starting point in his inquiries. If a view can explain and support these common beliefs, or, even better, if it can bring them into harmony with each other, that counts as an argument in its favor. In that spirit, I suggest that my view might be seen as a combination, or a welding together, of two other, more popular views that one often hears offered, if not as analyses of meaning in life, then at least as ingredients—sometimes the *key* ingredients—in a life well lived.

The first view tells us that it doesn't matter what you do with your life as long as it is something you love. Do not get stuck, or settle into doing something just because it is expected of you, or because it is conventionally recognized as good, or because nothing better occurs to you. Find your passion. Figure out what turns you on, and go for it.[4]

The second view says that in order to live a truly satisfying life one needs to get involved in something "larger than oneself."[5] The reference to the size of the group or the object

[3] Aristotle, *Topics* 1.1 100b 21–3. For an excellent discussion of the endoxic method, see Richard Kraut, "How to Justify Ethical Propositions: Aristotle's Method," in *The Blackwell Guide to Aristotle's "Nicomachean Ethics"* (Oxford: Blackwell, 2006) 76–95.

[4] One of those silly books that were on sale at the cashiers' desks at Barnes & Noble a few years ago advanced that view. The book, by Bradley Trevor Greive (Kansas City: Andrews McMeel Publishing, 2002) was called *The Meaning of Life*. Richard Taylor offers a more serious and provocative defense of the view in Richard Taylor, *Good and Evil* (New York: Macmillan, 1970), Chapter 18.

[5] Not surprisingly, it is common to hear religious leaders speak in these terms, but many others do as well. For example, Peter Singer draws on this conception of the good life in his book, *How Are We To Live? Ethics in an Age of Self-interest* (Melbourne: The Text Publishing Company, 1993).

one wants to benefit or be involved with is perhaps misleading and unfortunate, but it is not unreasonable to understand such language metaphorically, as a way of gesturing toward the aim of participating in or contributing to something whose value *is independent* of oneself. Understood this way, the first view, ("find your passion") may be understood as a way of advocating something similar to the subjective element contained in my proposed analysis of meaningfulness, while the second view, ("be part of something larger than yourself") urges us to satisfy the objective condition.

Each of these more popular views is sometimes couched in the vocabulary of meaning, and in each case there is a basis for that choice in our ordinary uses of the term. When thinking about one's own life, for example, a person's worry or complaint that his life lacks meaning is apt to be an expression of dissatisfaction with the subjective quality of that life. Some subjective good is felt to be missing. One's life feels empty. One longs to find something to do that will fill this gap and make one feel, as it were, fulfilled.

On the other hand, when we consider the lives of others, our tendency to characterize some as especially meaningful and others as less so is apt to reflect differences in our assessments of the objective value of what these lives are about. When we look for paradigms of meaningful lives, who comes to mind? Gandhi, perhaps, or Mother Theresa, or Einstein, or Cézanne. Sisyphus, condemned to an endless cycle of rolling a huge stone up a hill, only to have it roll down again, is a standard exemplar of a meaningless existence. Our choice of these examples seems to be based on the value (or lack of value) we take these people's activities to have, rather than on the subjective quality of their inner lives.

Insofar as the conception of meaningfulness I propose welds these two popular views together, it may be seen as a partial affirmation of both. From my perspective, both these views have something right about them, but each also leaves out something crucial.

Why believe any of these views? The question is ambiguous. Understood as the question, "Why believe that any one of these views offers a correct analysis of meaningfulness in life?" the inquiry seems to focus on whether any of the views under consideration captures a property or feature or set of conditions that answers to most of the instances in which the term "meaningful" is used in ordinary discourse, in contexts in which the topic in question is meaningfulness in life (as opposed, say, to meaningfulness in language). In answering this question, we would want to look at how the term *is* used in ordinary discourse: In what sorts of situations do questions of meaning arise? What sorts of concerns is the presence of meaning in a person's life supposed to put to rest? What types of lives would be generally accepted as paradigms of meaning? What types would be accepted as paradigms of meaninglessness? I have already expressed some doubt about whether there is a single cleanly definable concept that is being invoked in all the contexts in which talk of meaningful (and meaningless) lives may naturally take place. More important than the question of how to use the term "meaning," in any event, is the question of what a good life should contain. Above all, when therapists, ministers, and motivational speakers tell you either to "find your passion" or to "contribute to something larger than yourself," they are offering advice about how to live. More important than asking which, if any, of these views offers a plausible conception of "meaningfulness," is asking which, if any of them, identifies key and distinctive ingredients of a fully flourishing, successful, good life.

Still, it is difficult to keep the conceptual and the normative questions apart. Those who urge us to find our passions or to contribute to something larger than ourselves typically mean to be responding to a more particular set of concerns than is expressed by the general question, "How should one live?" We cannot properly interpret their advice, much less assess it, without having some idea of what those concerns are, and it would be difficult to call up the intuitions, to capture the images and feelings on which it is relevant to reflect, without occasionally using the word "meaningful" in our description. My own proposal, that we recognize a category of value that is not reducible to happiness or morality, and that is realized by loving objects worthy of love and engaging with them in a positive way, is offered as a refinement or as an alternative to these more popular forms of advice, and it is easiest to express this in terms that identify the category of value in question with meaningfulness. No harm, I hope, will be done by this. As long as we are alert to the possibility of filtering out questions about how to understand and apply the term "meaningful" from questions about what to aspire to in life, we can be careful to ensure that no questions will be begged.

The Fulfillment View

Let us turn our attention, then, to the first of the popular views I mentioned, the one that stresses the subjective element, urging each person to find his or her passion and pursue it. It is easy to see why someone would support this advice, and find plausible the claim that being able to pursue a passion adds something distinctive and deeply good to life. For the advice, at least as I understand it, rests on the plausible empirical supposition that doing what one loves doing, being involved with things one really cares about, gives one a kind of joy in life that one would otherwise be without. The reason one should find one's passion and go for it, then, is because doing so will give one's life a particular type of good feeling. Moreover, the distinctiveness of the type of good feeling in question makes it possible to see how the kind of life that engenders such feelings would be associated with meaningfulness, and how therefore one might be led to identify a meaningful life as a life lived pursuing one's passions.

Let us refer to the feelings one has when one is doing what one loves, or when one is engaging in activities by which one is gripped or excited, as feelings of fulfillment. Such feelings are the opposite of the very bad feelings of boredom and alienation. Although feelings of fulfillment are unquestionably good feelings, there are many other good feelings, perhaps more comfortably classified as pleasures, that have nothing to do with fulfillment. Riding a roller coaster, meeting a movie star, eating a hot fudge sundae, finding a great dress on sale, can all give one pleasure, even intense pleasure. They are unlikely to contribute to a sense of fulfillment, however, and it would not be difficult to imagine a person who has an abundance of opportunities for such pleasures still finding something (subjectively) lacking in her life.

Further, someone whose life is fulfilling has no guarantee of being happy in the conventional sense of that term. Many of the things that grip or engage us make us vulnerable to pain, disappointment, and stress. Consider, for example, writing a book, training for a triathlon, campaigning for a political candidate, caring for an ailing friend.

It may later be useful to bring to mind the fact that feelings of fulfillment are but one kind of positive feeling and potentially compete with other kinds: spending one's time, energy, money, and so on, on the projects that fulfill you necessarily reduces the resources you have for engaging in activities that are "merely" fun. Moreover, to the extent that one's sources of fulfillment are also sources of anxiety and suffering, the pleasure one gets from pursuing these things may be thought,

at least from a hedonistic perspective, to be qualified or balanced by the negative feelings that accompany it. Still, the
fact that most of us would willingly put up with a great deal
of stress, anxiety, and vulnerability to pain in order to pursue
our passions can be seen as providing support for the idea
that fulfillment is indeed a great and distinctive good in life.
Insofar as the view that urges us "to find our passion and go
for it" expresses that idea, there is a lot to be said for it. From
here on, I shall refer to that view as the "Fulfillment View."

Because feelings of fulfillment are different from and
sometimes compete with other types of good feeling, types
that are more paradigmatically associated with terms like
"happiness" and "pleasure," it is plausible to interpret the Fulfillment View as a proposal for what gives meaning to life.
To someone who finds himself puzzled by why, despite having a good job, a loving family, and a healthy body, he feels
that something is missing from his life, it provides an answer.
To someone trying to decide what career to pursue, or more
generally, how to structure his life, it advises against focusing
too narrowly on the superficial goals of ease, prestige, and
material wealth. Nonetheless, the Fulfillment View, as I have
interpreted it, is a form of hedonism, in that its prescription
for the best possible life (in which is included the possession
of meaning) rests exclusively on the question of how a life
can attain the best qualitative character. Positive experience
is, on this view, the only thing that matters.[6]

For this very reason, it seems to me, the view is inadequate
as it stands. If, as the Fulfillment View suggests, the only
thing that matters is the subjective quality of one's life, then

---

[6] The Fulfillment View might be considered a plausible extension of J. S. Mill's
view that an enlightened hedonist must take into account the differences in quality
as well as quantity of pleasure in conceiving of the best possible life. See John Stuart
Mill, *Utilitarianism* (1861), Chapter 2.

it shouldn't matter, in our assessments of possible lives, which activities give rise to that quality. If the point of finding one's passion and pursuing it is simply to be fulfilled—that is, to get and keep the *feelings* of fulfillment, then it shouldn't matter what activities or objects one has a passion for. Considering a variety of lives, all equally fulfilling, but differing radically in the sorts of things that give rise to that fulfillment, however, may make us wonder whether we can really accept that view.

Imagine, in particular, a person whose life is dominated by activities that most of us would be tempted to call worthless, but which nonetheless give fulfillment to that person. I earlier gave the example of a person who simply loves smoking pot all day, and another (or maybe the same person) who is fulfilled doing crossword puzzles, or worse (as personal experience will attest), Sudokus. We might also consider more bizarre cases: a man who lives to make handwritten copies of the text of *War and Peace*; or a woman whose world revolves around her love for her pet goldfish. Do we think that, from the point of view of self-interest, these lives are as good as can be—provided, perhaps, that their affections and values are stable, and that the goldfish doesn't die?

Initially, perhaps, not everyone will answer these questions in the same way; some will not know what to think. In part, I believe this is because we are uncomfortable making negative judgments about other people's lives, even about imaginary other people who are conceived realistically enough to be stand-ins for real people. We are especially uncomfortable making negative judgments that diverge from the judgments the characters would make about their own lives. To avoid this problem, let me approach these questions by way of reflection on a more stylized philosophical example—namely, the case of Sisyphus Fulfilled.

Sisyphus, in the ancient myth, is condemned to an existence that is generally acknowledged to be awful. He is condemned eternally to a task that is boring, difficult, and futile. Because of this, Sisyphus's life, or more precisely, his afterlife, has been commonly treated as a paradigm of a meaningless existence.[7]

The philosopher Richard Taylor, however, in a discussion of life's absurdity, suggests a thought experiment according to which the gods take pity on Sisyphus and inject a substance in his veins that transforms him from someone for whom stone-rolling is nothing but a painful, arduous, and unwelcome chore to someone who loves stone-rolling more than anything else in the (after-)world.[8] There is nothing the transformed Sisyphus would rather do than roll that stone. Stone-rolling, in other words, fulfills him. Sisyphus has found his passion (or perhaps his passion has found him), and he is pursuing it to his life's content. The question is, what should *we* think of him? Has his life been transformed from horribly unfortunate to exceptionally good? Taylor thinks so, but some of us might disagree.

As I have already noted, the reason Sisyphus has traditionally been taken as a paradigm of a meaningless existence is that he is condemned to the perpetual performance of a task that is boring, difficult, and futile. In Taylor's variation, Sisyphus's task is no longer boring—no longer boring to Sisyphus, that is. But it remains futile. There is no value to his efforts; nothing ever comes of them. Even if due to divine intervention, Sisyphus comes to enjoy and even to feel fulfilled by his activity, the pointlessness of what he is doing doesn't change.

[7] See especially Albert Camus, *The Myth of Sisyphus and Other Essays* (New York: Alfred A. Knopf, 1955).

[8] See Taylor, *Good and Evil* (n. 4, above).

In light of this, many will feel that Sisyphus's situation remains far from enviable. Something desirable seems missing from his life despite his experience of fulfillment. Since what is missing is not a subjective matter—from the inside, we may assume that Sisyphus's life is as good as can be—we must look for an objective feature that characterizes what is lacking. The second popular view I brought up earlier names, or at least gestures toward, a feature that might fit the bill.

The Larger-than-Oneself View and the Bipartite View

That second view tells us that the best sort of life is one that is involved in, or contributes to something "larger than oneself." Contemplation of the case of Sisyphus should, however, be enough to show that this "larger" must be understood metaphorically. We may, after all, imagine the rock Sisyphus is endlessly pushing uphill to be *very* large. We might rather understand the view as one that recommends involvement in something *more important* than ourselves—something, in other words, that is larger than ourselves not in size but in value. If the recommendation is to be taken as a criterion for a meaningful life, however, I would be inclined to argue against this interpretation, too. For one thing, if we assume that the value of one person's life is as great as the value of another's, it would seem to rule out the possibility that a life devoted to the care of a single other individual—a disabled partner, for example, or a frail, aging parent, or a child with special needs—could be a meaningful life, for the value of the one cared for is presumably just equal to and not larger than the value of the person who does the caring. When we try to assess projects and activities that are not principally aimed at the benefit of one or more human beings, the difficulties with such a view appear even more serious. Presumably, a dog is not more important than oneself—but what about two dogs, or six? And what about projects and activities that are not directed toward promoting anyone's welfare at all? Is philosophy or poetry or basketball something "larger than oneself" in value? It is difficult to know exactly what the question is asking.

A more promising interpretation of the view that links meaningfulness to involvement with something larger than oneself takes the metaphor of size less seriously. According to this interpretation, the point is to recommend that one get involved not with something larger than oneself, but rather with something *other* than oneself—that is, with something the value of which is independent of and has its source *outside of* oneself. Presumably, Sisyphean stone-rolling has no such value—nor, it seems, does pot-smoking or Sudoku-solving. But devotion to a single, needy individual does satisfy this condition as much as devotion to a crowd. Philosophy and basketball appear to meet this criterion, too, since the value of these activities, whatever it is, does not depend on one's own contingent interest in them.

If we interpret the advice that one get involved with something "larger than oneself" in this way, it might be thought to represent a second and independent criterion for a fully successful and flourishing life. Combining this advice with the Fulfillment View, one might think, yields a better, bipartite conception of meaningfulness than either view taken on its own. The Fulfillment View directs our attention to a subjective component that a meaningful life must contain. But, as the case of Sisyphus Fulfilled led us to see, even a life that fully satisfies the subjective condition may be one we would be hesitant to describe as meaningful, if objectively that life were unconnected to anything or anyone whose value lay outside of the person whose life it was. By conjoining the

Fulfillment View with the injunction to get involved with something "larger than oneself," we get a proposal that appears to remedy the problem. On this bipartite view, in order for a life to be meaningful both an objective and a subjective condition must be met: A meaningful life is a life that a.) the subject finds fulfilling, and b.) contributes to or connects positively with something the value of which has its source outside the subject.

If, however, meaningfulness is understood to refer to a coherent dimension of value, more specific than the general category of self-interest, or the even more general category of "all that is desirable in a life," it would be puzzling if it turned out to depend on the satisfaction of two unrelated conditions. The proposal I favor, which identifies meaning with a condition in which subjective and objective components are suitably linked, conceives of meaningfulness in a more unified way. My conception of meaningfulness sees subjective and objective elements fitting together to constitute a coherent feature a life might or might not possess. Besides, if we really consider the two conditions of meaningfulness proposed by the Bipartite View as criteria to be taken separately, it is not clear that they contribute to the goodness of a person's life at all.[9]

Consider again the suggestion that a life in which a person contributes to something larger than himself (suitably interpreted) is more meaningful than a life that serves only the needs and desires of the person whose life it is. I introduced this idea in answer to the question of what (desirable feature) might be missing from a life like that of Sisyphus Ful-

---

[9] I thank Cheshire Calhoun for pressing me to think about why the relation between the subjective and objective conditions of my conception of meaningfulness is important.

filled (or the pot-smoker, or Sudoku-player), that prevents it from representing a life we would want for ourselves or for those we love. We could add stipulations to these examples that guaranteed that the protagonists' lives and activities did contribute to some independent value. If they had no interest in the external or objective or independent value with which their lives were involved, however, it is not clear that that involvement would make their lives any better or more desirable to them. Imagine, for example, that unbeknownst to Sisyphus, his stone-rolling scares away vultures who would otherwise attack a nearby community and spread terror and disease. Or imagine that the pot-smoker's secondary marijuana smoke is alleviating the pain of the AIDS victim next door. If Sisyphus and the pot-smoker do not care about the benefits their lives are producing, it is hard to see why the fact that their lives yield those benefits—that they contribute, in other words, to something larger or other than themselves—should make us any more inclined to describe their lives as meaningful (or to find their lives desirable) than we were before we learned of these consequences.

Even when we consider people whose involvement with something "larger" is less accidental, the contribution this makes to the quality of their own lives is limited at best if they are not emotionally engaged with the people or things or activities that make what they are doing valuable. People who do valuable work but who cannot identify or take pride in what they are doing—the alienated housewife, the conscripted soldier, the assembly line worker, for example—may know that what they are doing is valuable, yet reasonably feel that their lives lack something that might be referred to as meaning.

In any case, it seems to me that when the recommendation to get involved with something larger than oneself is offered, it is offered in the hope, if not the expectation, that if one does get so involved, it will make one feel good. The thought is that if one tries it, one will like it, and one will like it in part because of one's recognition that one is engaged with a person or an object or an activity that is independently valuable.[10] The suggestion, then, that one gets meaning in life through involvement with something larger than oneself may be most charitably interpreted as a suggestion that is not meant to be taken in isolation. It is not to be regarded as a criterion of meaningfulness separable from any assumptions about the attitudes the subject will have toward the project or activity in question. If one gets involved in something larger than oneself—or, as I have interpreted it, in something the value of which is (in part) independent of oneself—then, if one is lucky, one will find that involvement fulfilling, and if that happens, then one's life will both be and seem meaningful. If one's involvement brings no such reward, however, it is unclear that it contributes to meaning in one's life at all.

Just as the objective condition sometimes associated with meaning—namely, that one's life be involved in something larger than oneself—is much more plausible when it is understood to function in conjunction with a positive subjective attitude to one's involvement, so it seems to me that the subjective condition—that one live in a way that one finds fulfilling—is more plausible when understood in conjunction with objective constraints. I suggested a moment ago that when someone recommends that you get involved in something larger than oneself, the hope, if not the expectation,

---

[10] This does not always work. It is a standard part of the requirements for a child who is training for a Bar or Bat Mitzvah, as it is for many middle and high school programs, that the child spend a specified number of hours engaged in community service. Not surprisingly, the degree to which this results in a gratifying experience, an enhanced social consciousness, or a lasting commitment varies widely.

that is lurking in the background is that you will find that involvement subjectively rewarding. Similarly, when someone recommends that you find your passion and go for it, there seems also to be a hope, if not an expectation, lurking in the background; namely, that the passion you find, the pursuit of which will be fulfilling, will be an intelligible one, within certain bounds. You will not be passionate—at least not for very long—about stone-rolling, or Sudokus, or caring for your goldfish, or making handwritten copies of *War and Peace.*

In my earlier discussion of Sisyphus Fulfilled, I expressed sympathy with those who, unlike Richard Taylor, found something desirable missing from Sisyphus's life, despite his being subjectively quite content. There is room for an even stronger disagreement with Taylor, however, that I want to consider now. Specifically, one might wonder whether the transformation that Sisyphus undergoes from being unhappy, bored, and frustrated to being blissfully fulfilled makes Sisyphus better off at all. One might think that it actually makes his situation worse.

From a hedonistic perspective, of course, Sisyphus's transformation *must* make his life better, for the only changes in Sisyphus are subjective. Negative feelings and attitudes are replaced by positive ones. From a nonhedonistic perspective, however, these changes come at a cost. When I try to understand the new Sisyphus's state of mind, when I try to imagine how someone might find stone-rolling fulfilling, I can only conceive of two possibilities: On the one hand, I can think of the substance in Sisyphus's veins as inducing delusions that make Sisyphus see something in stone-rolling that isn't really there. On the other hand, the drug in his veins may have lowered his intelligence and reduced his imaginative capacity, thus eliminating his ability to perceive the dullness and futility of his labors or to compare them to other more challenging or worthwhile things that, had the gods not condemned him, he might have been doing instead. In either case, Sisyphus is in at least one respect worse off than he was before his transformation. He is either afflicted by mental illness or delusions or diminished in his intellectual powers.

Opinion may divide over whether, all things considered, the transformation makes Sisyphus worse or better off. Those in strongest sympathy with Mill's claim that it is better to be a human unsatisfied than a pig satisfied may think that however bad the fate of the classical Sisyphus, the fate of the transformed Sisyphus is worse. Others may conclude that since Sisyphus is condemned to roll stones in any case, it is better for him to be happy with, or more precisely, fulfilled by his lot than otherwise. Even those who hold the view that it is better to be Sisyphus happy than Sisyphus unhappy, however, may agree that it is better still not to be Sisyphus at all.

To me, the first scenario, in which the transformed Sisyphus is deluded, seems a more plausible way to understand what it would be for Sisyphus to be or to feel *fulfilled* by stone-rolling, for "fulfillment" seems to me to include a cognitive component that requires seeing the source or object of fulfillment as being, in some independent way, good or worthwhile. Even deep and intense pleasures, like lying on the beach on a beautiful day, or eating a perfectly ripe peach, would not naturally be described as fulfilling. To find something fulfilling is rather to find it such as to be characterizable in terms that would portray it as (objectively) good.[11]

---

[11] Though he does not use the language of "fulfillment" and "meaningfulness," Stephen Darwall discusses the profound contribution to welfare that comes from "the experience of connecting with something of worth in a way that enables the direct appreciation of the value of one's activity" in, *Welfare and Rational Care* (Princeton: Princeton University Press, 2002) 95. His discussion of such experiences,

Imagining Sisyphus in terms of either scenario, however, can explain why we might hesitate to describe the life of Sisyphus Fulfilled as meaningful—and similarly, I would argue, why we would withhold that label from the life of the fulfilled pot-smoker, goldfish-lover, or Tolstoy-copier. Imagining these characters on the model of either scenario would, in any case, help to explain why we might regard their lives as far from ideal. Earlier I suggested that we might judge these lives to be "missing something," a phrase that suggests a feature separable from fulfillment that these lives lack, rendering them less than optimally meaningful (if meaningful at all). In light of our discussion, we can now see that even the apparent condition of meaningfulness they do satisfy—that is, the condition of being fulfilled—is in a certain way defective and less desirable than fulfillment stemming from a more fitting or appropriate source.

The Fitting Fulfillment View Defended

I earlier argued that the suggestion that a life is meaningful insofar as it contributes to something larger than itself is most charitably understood if we take it not as an isolated objective criterion; rather, we should see it as a criterion that functions in tandem with an expectation about the subjective feelings and attitudes that contributing to something larger will engender. Analogously, the suggestion that a life is meaningful insofar as one finds one's passion and goes for it (thereby being fulfilled) is best understood as a subjective criterion meant to function not in isolation but rather in

---

which I take to be more or less identical to what I am describing as experiences of fulfillment, offers an especially good characterization of the kind of appreciation of value at issue that avoids over-intellectualizing it. The account of human welfare he develops in Chapter Four has much in common with the description of meaningfulness I defend here.

conjunction with the assumption that the objects of one's passions will fall within a certain objective range.

The conception of meaningfulness that I proposed at the beginning of this lecture brings these two criteria together. That conception, you will remember, claimed that meaningfulness in life came from loving something (or a number of things) worthy of love, and being able to engage with it (or them) in some positive way. As I have put it on other occasions, meaning in life consists in and arises from actively engaging in projects of worth.[12] On this conception, meaning in life arises when subjective attraction meets objective attractiveness, and one is able to do something about it or with it.

The popular view that takes meaningfulness to consist in finding one's passion and pursuing it can be taken as a way to emphasize the role that love, or subjective attraction, plays in meaning. The equally familiar view that associates meaning with a contribution to or involvement with something larger than oneself can be understood as emphasizing the role of objective value or worth. The endoxic method thus supports the conception of meaningfulness I propose here. It supports the view that when people talk about meaningfulness, they often have roughly the thing I have identified in mind; it supports the idea that the feature I have identified is, at some level, recognized as desirable; that it is thought, or perhaps better, *felt* to answer to a certain kind of human need. The question remains, however, why such a feature should be thought or felt to be desirable. What, if anything, is so good,

[12] See Susan Wolf, "The Meanings of Lives," in *Introduction to Philosophy: Classical and Contemporary Readings*, eds. John Perry, Michael Bratman, and John Martin Fischer (New York: Oxford University Press, 2007) 62–73; and Susan Wolf, "Meaningful Lives in a Meaningless World," *Quaestiones Infinitae* 19 (June 1997), publication of the Department of Philosophy, Utrecht University, 1–22. This formulation fails to emphasize the element of love (or passion or identification) as much as the others.

so *distinctively* good, about loving objects worthy of love and being able actively to engage with them in a positive way? An advantage of my conception of meaning, in addition to its being supported by the endoxic method, is that it identifies a feature that yields an intelligible and plausible answer to this question.

We have already noted that being able to be actively engaged with things that one loves, being able, in other words, to indulge one's passions, affords a particularly rewarding type of subjective experience—it is, if you will, a high quality pleasure. Like the Fulfillment View, the Fitting Fulfillment View (for lack of a better name) identifies a feature that gives this recognizable benefit to the person whose life possesses it. According to the latter view, however, what is distinctively valuable is not the state or ongoing experience of fulfillment considered in itself. Rather, what is valuable is that one's life be actively (and lovingly) engaged in projects that give rise to this feeling, when the projects in question can be seen to have a certain kind of objective worth. It is not enough, on this view, that one is occupied with doing things that one loves. The things one loves doing must be good in some independent way. Why should this be something that matters to us? If having this in one's life answers a human need, what human need is it?

At least part of the answer, I believe, has to do with a need, or at least an interest or concern, to see one's life as valuable in a way that can be recognized from a point of view other than one's own. We can better understand this need, and perhaps quell the doubts of those who are skeptical of its existence, if we see its connection to other features of human psychology with which we are familiar from other contexts.

One such feature that has long been of interest to philosophers has been especially emphasized by Thomas Nagel

—namely, the human capacity, indeed the tendency, to see (or try to see) oneself from an external point of view.[13] Humans have a tendency to aspire to see things, including themselves, without bias, to observe their lives from a detached perspective. They aspire to a kind of objectivity. Nagel has characterized this as an aspiration to take a "view from nowhere"; others have talked about this feature in terms of a God's-eye point of view.

In addition, humans have a need to think well of themselves—a need for self-esteem. If one is prone to imagine oneself from an external point of view, to see oneself as if from without, the wish quite naturally follows that from that point of view one will be able to see oneself and one's life as good, valuable, and a rightful source of pride.

Still, the strength of that wish, and the peculiarly poignant feelings that can accompany it seem to me to involve something further, that, I suggest, is related to our social natures, and to our need or wish not to be alone.

Contemplation of one's mortality or of one's cosmic insignificance can call up the sort of feelings I have in mind. The thought that one's life is like a bubble that, upon bursting, will vanish without a trace can lead some people to despair. The thought that one lives in an indifferent universe makes some people shudder. Reminding oneself of the fact, if it is a fact, that one is actively and, we may stipulate, somewhat successfully, engaged in projects of independent worth may put these feelings to rest. By living in a way that is partly occupied by and directed toward the preservation or promotion or creation of value that has its source outside of oneself, one does something that can be understood, admired or

---

[13] See especially Thomas Nagel, *The View from Nowhere* (New York: Oxford University Press, 1986).

appreciated from others' points of view, including the imaginary point of view of an impartial indifferent observer.[14]

The fact that the feature focused on by the Fitting Fulfillment View can have bearing on our reactions to thoughts about the human condition, that it can even offer some solace to those who are distressed when they think about our insignificance, gives some support to the idea that this feature is reasonably identified with "meaningfulness," since it makes the association between meaningfulness and the age-old philosophical topic of "the meaning of life" more than a coincidence.

A longing for fulfillment, and an admiration for lives engaged in projects that are fitting for fulfillment, are not restricted to times when we are especially cognizant of the human condition, however. Even when we are not thinking about our relation to the cosmos, we may intelligibly want to do something whose value extends beyond its value *for us*. Indeed, even if we never explicitly formulate a desire that our lives be connected to something of independent value, the unarticulated *sense* that we are so connected may affect the quality of our experience. The *feeling* of being occupied with something of independent value, the engagement in an activity that takes one out of oneself, it seems to me, can be thrilling. Why? At least part of the reason, again, seems to be related to our social natures, and our desire not to be alone. If we are engaged in projects of independent value—fighting injustice, preserving a historic building, writing a

[14] Of course, there is no guarantee that such a thought *will* put the feelings in question to rest. Many people are upset by the thought that they are mere specks in a vast universe. They are upset, that is, by their smallness, their inability to make a big and lasting splash. My remarks—aimed at reminding them of the quality, not the quantity, of their contribution to the universe—do not speak directly to this concern. Such people will just have to get over it. Their desire is unsatisfiable. For further discussion of this topic, see my "The Meanings of Lives" (fn 12, above).

poem—then presumably others will be able to appreciate what we are doing, too. Others may actually appreciate what we are doing, or they may at least appreciate the same values as the ones that motivate us. This makes us at least notionally part of a community, sharing values to some degree and a point of view. Even when no one knows what we are doing, or when no one appreciates it, however, the thought that it is worth doing can be important to us. The scorned artist or lonely inventor, the scientist whose research no one seems to approve, may be sustained by the thought that her work is good, and that the day may come when others will understand and value it.[15]

Although I have suggested that the desirability of living in a positive relation with something the value of which does not depend solely on ourselves is related to our sociability, these last examples show that the relation may be indirect, perhaps even metaphorical. People who, for any number of reasons, cannot or do not wish to live around or be in intimate contact with other people, may still live meaningful and fulfilling lives. Some artists, for example, may make art for an only dimly conceived posterity. Conversely, for some people, the support, approval, and admiration of their contemporaries is not enough to make them feel fulfilled by what they are doing, or to judge their own lives as meaningful.

It may be suspected that the interests I am discussing are bourgeois interests, commonly of concern only to persons from a certain place, time, and social class. Perhaps it will be

---

[15] These remarks, I think, add to the plausibility of interpreting popular references to being involved in something "larger than oneself" in terms of the idea that one should be engaged with a value that has its source outside of oneself. The thought is that such a value exists metaphorically in a public space—it is accessible to others, and so makes one at the least a potential member of a community that is larger than oneself.

thought that these concerns are confined to a class that is narrower still; namely, to those who are excessively intellectual or unusually reflective. If one has to struggle to get enough to eat for oneself and one's family, to get shelter from the cold, to fight a painful disease, concern over whether one is engaged in projects of independent worth may seem a luxury. The fact that an interest in a meaningful life may not surface until one's more basic needs are met is no reason to dismiss its importance, however. Nor does it seem to me that the fact that a person does not consciously articulate an interest in ensuring that some of the projects or things with which his life is bound up can be judged to have independent worth is enough to warrant the view that whether they have such worth is irrelevant to him. Bernard Williams once wrote, with respect to the question of life's being desirable, that "it gets by far its best answer in never being asked at all."[16] Similarly, I think, for a person whose life is meaningful, the need to think about it might never come up. If a person is actively engaged in valuable projects, he may be getting feedback from these projects that enhances his life even if he is unaware of it.

Our interest in being able to see our lives as worthwhile from some point of view external to ourselves, and our interest in being able to see ourselves as part of an at least notional community that can understand us and that to some degree shares our point of view, then, seem to me to be pervasive, even if not universal. By engaging in projects of independent value, by protecting, preserving, creating, and realizing value the source of which lies outside of ourselves, we can satisfy these interests. Indeed, it is hard to see how we could satisfy them in any other way.

[16] Bernard Williams, "The Makropulos Case: Reflections on the Tedium of Immortality," in *Problems of the Self* (Cambridge: Cambridge University Press, 1973) 87.

Reflecting on the pervasiveness of these interests, and on the way a life of "fitting fulfillment" answers to them will, I hope, support both my proposal that meaningfulness is a matter of active and loving engagement in projects of worth and my claim that this feature, distinct from both happiness and morality, deserves to be included in a conception of a fully successful human life.

For much of this lecture, I have stressed the subjective aspect of a meaningful life—that is, the aspect that assures a meaningful life of being fulfilling, and to that extent feeling good. This emphasis brought out what my view of meaningfulness has in common with the more popular Fulfillment View (the view that says one should find one's passion, and go for it) and allowed me easily to demonstrate one way in which a meaningful life was good for the person who lives it. When we consider what deep human interests or needs a meaningful life *distinctively* answers to, however, the objective aspect of such a life needs to be stressed. Our interest in living a meaningful life is not an interest in a life *feeling* a certain way, but rather an interest that it *be* a certain way, specifically, that it be one that can be appropriately appreciated, admired, or valued by others;[17] that it be a life that contributes to or realizes or connects in some positive way with independent value. We do not satisfy those interests simply by thinking or feeling that they are satisfied any more than we can satisfy our interest in not being alone by thinking or feeling that we are not alone. To have a life that not only

[17] This is not unrelated to the interest in our actions being "justifiable to others" that Thomas Scanlon stresses in his account of the motivation and reason to be moral. See, *e.g.*, T. M. Scanlon, *What We Owe To Each Other* (Cambridge: Harvard University Press, 1998). The interest I have in mind, to which meaning rather than morality answers, however, is broader, embracing not only the possible points of view of one's fellow human beings, but the imaginable point of view of an even more external, nonhuman observer.

seems meaningful but is meaningful, the objective aspect is as important as the subjective.

Many questions about this conception of meaningfulness and its importance remain, however. In particular, I have not yet addressed, or even so much as acknowledged, the resistance many readers are no doubt feeling toward my references to objective value, or to the corresponding view that some activities or projects are more fitting than others to be the objects of one's life's central passions. I shall begin the next lecture by responding to these concerns. Let me warn you in advance, though, that I shall not be offering a *theory* of objective value, much less a foolproof procedure for determining which things have it. In light of this, one might reasonably wonder why I bother to bring up the subject at all. The remainder of the second lecture will be aimed at answering that question. By the end of the second lecture, then, I shall have tried to convince you not only of what meaning is, but also of why it matters.

Why It Matters

IN THE PREVIOUS LECTURE, I argued that philosophical models of human psychology that divide all motives and reasons into the self-interested and the moral, or the personal and the impersonal, were simplistic and distorting, failing to capture the character of our relationships with many of the things and activities that are most important to us. Further, I claimed that insofar as such models encourage us to think about our lives in terms only of happiness and morality, they lead us to neglect another important dimension along which lives can be better or worse—namely, the dimension of meaningfulness.

But what is meaningfulness? I argued in the last lecture for a conception that combined aspects of two popular views. Like the Fulfillment View, which tells us to find our passions and pursue them, my view acknowledges a subjective component in the meaningful life. A person who is alienated from her life, who gets no joy or pride from the activities that comprise it, can be said to lack meaning in her life. Like the view that associates meaning with involvement in something "larger than oneself," however, my view also recognizes an objective component. According to what I called the Fitting Fulfillment View, a life is meaningful insofar as its subjective attractions are to things or goals that are objectively worthwhile. That is, one's life is meaningful insofar as one finds oneself loving things worthy of love and able to do something positive about it. A life is meaningful, as I also put it, insofar as it is actively and lovingly engaged in projects of worth.

Throughout most of its history, moral philosophy has ignored the dimension of meaningfulness. Indeed, most philosophers have failed to notice it altogether. In this lecture I shall bring out some of the costs of this neglect. But before turning to this topic, there is some unfinished business to address.

My abstract characterization of meaningfulness leaves many questions open and many challenges unanswered. Not surprisingly, perhaps, the most pressing questions and most serious challenges have to do with the "objective" side of the proposal; that is, with the category I have variously referred to in terms of fittingness (for fulfillment), worthiness (of love), and independent, as well as objective, value. Which projects, one wants to know, are fitting for fulfillment? Which objects are worthy of love? How does one determine whether an activity is fitting or worthy or of independent value? For that matter, why accept the legitimacy of these judgments at all?

These questions raise issues that go to the heart of my proposal. If there is no such thing as (the relevant kind of) objective value, or if talk of distinctions in worth is nonsensical, then meaning in life, as I understand it, is impossible. These issues, then, are too central to my conception of meaningfulness for me not to acknowledge them here. Although, as you will see, my answers to all these questions are tentative, I do not think this is a reason to be skeptical of the conception of meaningfulness that evokes them.

After elaborating and defending my views on these matters, I shall turn finally to the topic promised in this lecture's title; namely, to the question of why it matters, especially in light of the tentativeness, vagueness, and openness of the category under discussion, that we think of life's possibilities in terms not only of happiness and morality but in terms of meaning as well.

Questions about Objective Value

To address the first set of questions, let me begin at an untheoretical, or what many philosophers refer to as an intuitive, level. It will be useful to recall from the previous lecture that the idea that there must be some objective condition on the kinds of projects or passions that could form the basis of a meaningful life arose in connection with the observation that some projects, such as rolling a stone uselessly up a hill, making handwritten copies of *War and Peace*, solving Sudoku puzzles, or caring for one's pet goldfish, were in some way inadequate. By noting what is lacking from such projects, we can form hypotheses about what features make an activity more fitting as a grounding for meaning. As many of the problematic cases cited seem to exemplify useless activity, it seems plausible to propose that activities that are useful are to that extent better candidates for grounding claims of meaningfulness. And, as many involve activities that are routinized or mechanical—in other words, activities that would be boring to a normal human being of moderate intelligence and ability—we may conjecture that an activity's or project's suitability as a meaning-provider rises as it becomes more challenging, or as it offers greater opportunity for a person to develop her powers or realize her potential.

It is noteworthy what a broad and diverse range of projects and activities meet these standards. In particular, though it will include the projects and activities recognized as morally valuable by conventional standards, embracing both positive relationships with family and friends and engagement with political and social causes, the range extends far beyond that. Creating art, adding to our knowledge of the world, preserving a place of natural beauty all seem intuitively to deserve classification as valuable activities, even if they do not bring about obvious improvement in human or animal welfare. So do efforts to achieve excellence or to develop one's powers—for example, as a runner, a cellist, a cabinetmaker, a pastry chef.

It is in part because the range of activities that seem to qualify as fitting for fulfillment, and so as able to ground claims of meaningfulness, is so large and so varied that the words I have used to characterize this condition are so general and so vague. Perhaps the best of the expressions I have used in this connection is that which says that the project or activity must possess a value whose source comes from outside of oneself—whose value, in other words, is in part independent of one's own attitude to it. That expression has the advantage of being minimally exclusive. It makes the point that a project whose only value comes from its being pleasing, or interesting, or fulfilling to the person whose project it is—a project, that is, whose value is entirely individually subjective—is not the kind of project that can make a person's life meaningful, but it makes no other restrictions as to either the kind or the source of value the project or activity may have. Intuitively, however, this condition may be *too* minimal if taken literally. When we imagine lives in which various sorts of activities play prominent roles, with an eye to their meaningfulness, some sort of proportionality condition seems to operate in the background. Strictly speaking, it may not be right to say of the woman whose life revolves around her pet goldfish, or of the man who painstakingly copies *War and Peace* by hand, that their activities have *no* value independent of their own psychologies. Perhaps the life and comfort of a goldfish is worth *something* independently, as is an extra copy of a literary masterpiece, easily available in libraries and bookstores though it be. Even so, the corresponding endeavors do not seem valuable *enough* to merit the kind of time, energy, and investment that these characters are imagined to devote to them, particularly in light of the wealth of other possible activities that we assume they might be engaging with instead.

Furthermore, there seems good reason to ask why, if an activity's value to *oneself* is insufficient to give meaning to one's life, an activity's value to some *other* creature should make it any more suitable. Are we to understand the condition that an activity be of value "independent of oneself" to be met by anything that is of value to another (in the sense of being enjoyed by, or of use to her)? If, in addition to Sisyphus, a third party was pleased or fulfilled by watching Sisyphus roll stones up a hill, or if, in addition to the goldfish owner, all the woman's neighbors were deeply concerned about the well-being of her pet, would that make a difference in the assessment of these lives as meaningful? If so, it is puzzling why this should be so significant. If not, the condition of "independent value" stands in need of further specification.

To make matters worse, the difficulty of answering these questions may begin to make one wonder whether we should accept any such condition at all. Despite the discomfort we may have with the idea that the lives of the goldfish lover, the Tolstoy copier, and the satisfied Sisyphus are meaningful, perhaps we should resist the temptation to exclude them by way of a condition of fittingness or a requirement of worth. There are two sorts of reasons that tend to fuel such suspicions, and they are worth distinguishing and responding to separately. On the one hand, there are worries of a moral, or quasi-moral nature, having to do with the dangers of parochialism and elitism. On the other, there are philosophical concerns about the metaphysics of value.

Who's to Say? The Danger of Elitism

The first set of concerns is important, and expressive of values that I wholeheartedly support, but I believe their acknowledgement is wholly compatible with the spirit and intention of the view I am presenting. I have in mind concerns that might most naturally be expressed by the rhetorical question, "*Who's to say?—Who's to say* which projects are fitting (or worthy or valuable) and which are not?" The worry is that the views of any one person or any group that sets itself up as an authority on values are liable to be narrow-minded or biased. No doubt the examples I use to illustrate my views, reflective as they are of my bourgeois American values, make this concern all the more salient.

To be sure, elitism and parochialism *are* dangers that we need to be wary of, especially perhaps when making judgments about the relative value of what other people do with their lives. But we can minimize these dangers if we keep our fallibility in mind, if we regard our judgments as tentative, and if we remind ourselves, when necessary, that the object of thinking about the category of meaningfulness in life is not to produce a meaningfulness scale for ranking lives.

To the question, "Who's to say which projects are independently valuable and which are not?" my answer is, "No one in particular." Neither I, nor any group of professional ethicists or academicians—nor, for that matter, any other group I can think of—have any special expertise that makes their judgment particularly reliable. Rather, questions like, "Which projects are valuable?" and "Which activities are worthwhile?" are open to anyone and everyone to ask and to try to answer, and I assume that we will answer them better if we pool our information, our experience, and our thoughts. Our initial pretheoretical or intuitive judgments about what is valuable and what is a waste of time are formed in childhood, as a result of a variety of lessons, experiences, and other cultural influences. Being challenged to justify our judgments, being exposed to different ones, broadening our range of experience, and learning about other cultures and ways of life will lead us to revise, and, if all goes well, improve our judgments. Presumably, this is a never-ending enterprise, not only because, as fallible creatures, our judgments of value will always be somewhat tentative, but also because the sorts of things that have value are apt to change over time. If the history of the arts is any model for the history of value more generally, human ingenuity and a continually changing universe will ensure that new forms of value will evolve.[1] Perhaps old ones will atrophy as well. The absence of a final authority on the question of which things have value, however, does not call into doubt the legitimacy or coherence of the question itself or of the enterprise of trying to find a more or less reasonable, if also partial, tentative, and impermanent answer.

Two Kinds of Subject-independent Value

The second set of concerns to which I earlier referred does call the category of objective value into doubt. Whereas worries about elitism call our attention to the dangers of thinking one knows *which* things, activities, or projects have value, the second set of concerns, more purely philosophical, raises

---

[1] See Joseph Raz, *The Practice of Value* (Oxford: Oxford University Press, 2003) 33. He writes, "As art forms, social relations and political structures are created by social practices . . . so must their distinctive virtues and forms of excellence depend on social practices that create and sustain them. In these cases, it would seem that not only access to these values, but the values themselves, arise with the social forms that make their instantiation possible."

questions about the idea that there is such a thing as an objective standard of value at all, or more precisely, an objective standard that distinguishes some projects, activities, and interests from others as being more fitting for or more capable of contributing to the meaningfulness of one's life.

In addressing these concerns, it is important to keep in mind what kinds of objectivity are at issue, for the term is notoriously slippery. In the context at hand, the reference to objectivity can be associated with two very different ways in which, in order for a project to be capable of contributing to the meaning of a person's life, its value must be at least partly independent of that person.

One way is suggested by the grain of truth to be found in the popular view that one's life gets meaning from engagement with something "larger than oneself," at least if, as I argued in the last lecture, we can understand this to refer more literally to the condition that one must be in some positive relationship with things or activities the value of which lies at least partly *outside* of oneself. A central thought here seems to be that a life lacks meaning if it is totally egocentric, devoted solely toward the subject's own survival and welfare, and realizing no value that is independent of the subject's own good. Meaning comes rather from successful engagement with values that are not just values *for* the person herself—for only then, it seems, will one be able to say that one has lived in a way that can be claimed to be worthwhile from a point of view external and potentially indifferent to oneself.

From a certain perspective, it may seem puzzling that while a life devoted to oneself, and realizing no value that is independent of oneself, is to be regarded as meaningless, a life engaged positively with some other person or creature or valuable activity has meaning. If finding food and shelter for one's child, nursing one's partner back to health, rescuing one's wounded comrade from the hands of death, are worthwhile activities, why shouldn't feeding, sheltering, healing, and rescuing *oneself* be worthwhile as well? It may seem odd that if I benefit you and you benefit me, our activities may contribute to the meaningfulness of each other's lives, but if we each tend to our own well-being, our actions will have no such effect.

This puzzle disappears, however, when we recall the distinctiveness of the category of meaningfulness and recognize that activities, projects, or actions may be valuable in some way without being valuable in a way that contributes to meaningfulness. Certainly, if there is value in saving another person's life, there is value in saving one's own; certainly, taking care of oneself, seeking happiness, and avoiding pain, are sensible and worthwhile things to do. It can even be perfectly reasonable to do a Sudoku puzzle once in a while, or to keep a goldfish. But whether a life is meaningful has specifically to do with whether one's life can be said to be worthwhile from an external point of view. A meaningful life is one that would not be considered pointless or gratuitous, even from an impartial perspective. Living in a way that connects positively with objects, people, and activities that have value independent of oneself harmonizes with the fact that one's own perspective and existence have no privileged status in the universe. This is why engagement with things that have value independent of oneself can contribute to the meaningfulness of one's life in a way that activities directed at one's own good and valuable in no other way do not.[2]

The notion that some of the things that engage us have nonsubjective value in this sense—value, that is, that is not

---

[2] For an extended discussion of this point, see my "The Meanings of Lives" and "Meaningful Lives in a Meaningless World" (Lecture One, fn 12, above).

just value for the subject—is not metaphysically mysterious or conceptually problematic. It is easy enough, at least in principle, to distinguish activities that are valuable only to oneself from those that are not. It is good *for me* that I get to eat fine chocolates, or watch *Friday Night Lights*, or take a walk in the woods, but no one else in the world is benefited by these things, nor is any independent value realized or produced. By contrast, what good there is in my helping someone else, or even in my writing a good book, is not exclusively goodness for me. What values there are in these activities are at least partly independent of my own existence and point of view.

There is, however, another kind of subject-independence that is more philosophically problematic and has more to do with traditional worries about the metaphysics of value. Specifically, in order for one's activities or projects to contribute to the meaningfulness of one's life, not only must the locus or recipient of value lie partly outside of oneself, the standard of judgment for determining value must be partly independent, too. According to the Fitting Fulfillment View, thinking or feeling that one's life is meaningful doesn't make it so, at least not all by itself. One can be mistaken about whether a project or activity has the kind of value necessary to make it a potential provider of meaning.

Examples I gave yesterday, like Sisyphus Fulfilled, were meant to suggest the conceivability of a person finding an activity fulfilling that we might find inadequate for meaning from a third-person perspective. Insofar as (this version of) Sisyphus thinks his life is meaningful, he is mistaken, finding something in stone-rolling that isn't really there. Realistic examples may be more controversial, but they are easy enough to find: On drugs, one may find counting bathroom tiles fascinating, or one may watch reruns of *Father Knows*

Best with rapture. A member of a religious cult may think that obedience to her leader's commands and dedication to his empowerment are worthwhile goals. An attorney fresh out of law school may see his ardent defense of an unscrupulous corporate client as a noble expression of justice in action; a personal assistant to a Hollywood star may be seduced by the glitter and fame that surround her into thinking that catering to her employer's every whim is a matter of national significance. Such people may think a life devoted to the advancement of their goals and heroes is a meaningful one. They may feel fulfilled by activities that foster what they take to be worthwhile ends. But, according to the Fitting Fulfillment View, they would be mistaken.

The judgment that what seemed worthwhile wasn't really so may be made by the person himself, looking back on a past phase of his existence. One might even "wake up" more or less suddenly to the realization that an activity one has been pursuing with enthusiasm is shallow or empty. As these examples make plausible the idea that a person may find meaning in an activity that really isn't there, other examples suggest the converse possibility: We can imagine Bob Dylan's mother thinking her son was wasting his time messing around with that guitar; or Fred Astaire's father wishing his son would quit dancing and get a real job. Tolstoy went through a period when he could not see the value of his own literary accomplishments, magnificent as they were. The realization that he had done much that had made his life meaningful was unavailable to him. These examples suggest that a person may judge an activity to be worthless that others can see to be valuable. With respect to negative as well as positive judgments of value, it appears that one can be wrong.

If we accept the idea that a person's judgment about the value of an activity can be wrong, then we accept the legitimacy of a kind of value judgment that is subject-independent.[3] According to the conception of meaningfulness I am proposing, that sort of judgment is essential to understanding what a meaningful life is.

Problems with the Metaphysics of Value

Accepting the legitimacy of this type of subject-independent value judgment and thereby denying radical subjectivism with respect to value, seems a far cry from accepting the sort of metaphysically mysterious conception of objective value sometimes associated with Plato or more recently with G. E. Moore. To acknowledge that a person may be mistaken about what has value, and that finding something valuable doesn't necessarily make it so, is hardly to commit oneself to a view that value is a nonnatural property, or that, as John Mackie has put it, it is built into "the fabric of the world."[4] Nor does believing that one can be mistaken about value, or even that everyone can be mistaken about value, imply that values might even in principle be independent of human (or other conscious beings') needs and capacities.

There are many accounts of value that fall in between the radically subjective and the radically objective. In claiming that meaningfulness has an objective component, (that certain projects and not others are fitting for fulfillment; certain objects worthy of love, and so on), I mean only to insist that something other than a radically subjective account of value must be assumed. Nonetheless, I must confess that I have no positive account of nonsubjective value with which I am satisfied. Radically objective accounts of value are implausible

---

[3] That is, the truth of the judgment that an activity is worthwhile is independent of whether a subject, such as Tolstoy or Sisyphus, thinks that the activity is worthwhile.

[4] J. L. Mackie, *Ethics: Inventing Right and Wrong* (Harmondsworth: Penguin, 1977).

and obscure, but the most obvious conceptions of value that fall between those and the radically subjective are problematic as well.

Thus, for example, some people are attracted to intersubjective accounts, according to which whether something is valuable depends on whether it is valued by a community of valuers. If an individual's valuing something isn't sufficient to give the thing real value, however, it is hard to see why a group's endorsement should carry any more weight. If one person can be mistaken about value, why can't five people, or five thousand? The history of art, or for that matter of morals, seems ample testimony to the view that whole societies can be wrong.

More promising, I think, are accounts that link value to the hypothetical responses of an idealized individual or group. Whether something is valuable on such a view is associated with the claim that it *would* be valued by someone sufficiently rational, perceptive, sensitive, and knowledgeable, to be, as John Stuart Mill would say, "a competent judge."[5] Yet this view, too, seems inadequate as it stands, for if it is interpreted as claiming that what *makes* something valuable is its being able to evoke such a reaction in such an individual, the view needs further explanation and defense. Why should an object's capacity to be valued by an imaginary individual make the object valuable if its being actually valued by me or my friends or my fellow countrymen does not? If, on the other hand, the reference to these hypothetical responses is understood as a way to track value rather than as an account of what constitutes it, then the view seems to leave the question with which we are most concerned—the question of what is being tracked (or, if you will, of what value is)—untouched.

[5] John Stuart Mill, *Utilitarianism* (1861), Chapter 2.

On my view, then, finding an adequate account of the objectivity of values—that is, of the ways or respects in which value judgments are not radically subjective—is an unsolved problem in philosophy, or perhaps better, an unsolved cluster of problems. Though I believe we have good reason to reject a radically subjective account of value, it is far from clear what a reasonably complete and defensible nonsubjective account will look like.

The absence of such an account gives us all the more reason to be tentative in our judgments about what sorts of project deserve inclusion in the class of activities that can contribute to the meaningfulness of a life. We must admit the reasonableness of controversy not only about the value of particular activities, such as cheerleading, ultimate Frisbee, and analytic philosophy, but also about whole categories of activity, such as aesthetic expression, self-realization, or communion with nature. My own inclination is to be generous in my assumptions about what is valuable in the sense required to qualify as a potential contributor to meaning. I expect that almost anything that a significant number of people have *taken* to be valuable over a long span of time is valuable. If people find an object or activity or project engaging, there is apt to be something about it that makes it so—perhaps the activity is challenging, the object beautiful, the project morally important.

Still, these expectations may not be supportable. A quick glance at the *Guinness Book of World Records* or at a list of internet chat rooms will remind one that people, indeed, large numbers of people, do the darnedest things. They race lawn mowers, compete in speed-eating contests, sit on flagpoles, watch reality TV. Do these activities merit the investment of time and money that people put into them? Do they contribute to the meaning of these people's lives? There may be something to be said on both sides of these questions.

As some will have been critical of my endorsement of the idea of nonsubjective value and the associated thought that such value distinguishes some projects from others as more or less able to contribute to a meaningful life, others will be frustrated or annoyed by my reluctance confidently to apply the notion, to make substantive judgments that actually identify meaningful projects, and to contrast them to meaningless ones. If you are unwilling to take a stand on *which* lives are meaningful, they might ask, why bother discussing the subject at all? What is the point of insisting that there is such a thing as a meaningful life if you cannot give any kind of guidance for how to live one? Why, in other words, in light of your caution in attributing meaning or the lack of meaning to specific concrete lives, does recognizing the abstract category of meaningfulness matter?

Why It (the Concept of Meaningfulness) Matters

An answer we might consider is that, even without being able to say anything more systematic or definite about meaningfulness, the mere reference to it as an explicit element of what is to be desired and aimed for in life may make us more likely to attain it than we would otherwise be. After all, even if we don't have a good philosophical account or theory about which projects, activities, and interests possess the kind of nonsubjective value that makes them potential contributors to meaning in our lives, we are not totally clueless about these matters in practice. The mere mention of meaningfulness might remind a person at least to notice whether his life is (or seems to be) satisfying in this respect, and this may be enough to make a difference in the shape he gives to it.

I would not place too much weight on this suggestion, however. Many, perhaps most, people manage to live meaningful lives without giving the *idea* of meaning a moment's explicit thought, and those whose lives are not satisfactorily meaningful are not likely to be able to remedy this shortfall simply by having it called more explicitly to their attention.[6]

If our lives or the lives of our students and our children are to become more meaningful as a result of thinking about meaningfulness, this will more likely happen by an indirect route. The immediate benefits of thinking abstractly about meaningfulness are apt to be more purely intellectual. Specifically, attention to the category of meaningfulness may help us to better understand our values and ourselves and may enable us to better assess the role that some central interests and activities play in our lives.

In fact, much of what I think is valuable about thinking about meaningfulness has to do with thinking about what meaningfulness is *not*. At the beginning of the previous lecture, I remarked that it is not (equivalent to) happiness, and it is not (equivalent to) morality. Recognizing that meaning is something desirable in life, something we want both for ourselves and for others, means recognizing that there is more to life than either of these categories, even taken together, suggests. This means, among other things, that it need not be irrational to choose to spend one's time doing something that neither maximizes one's own good nor is morally best.

Moreover, realizing that there are things worth doing that do not contribute maximally to either happiness or morality may change the way we understand these concepts themselves.

---

[6] Many people, through no fault of their own, simply lack the opportunity for meaning: their physical, economic, or political circumstances deprive them of the freedom or the leisure to explore and pursue activities they would love. Others may have temperaments that make it difficult to love anything in the right sort of way. One cannot find something engaging at will.

As I mentioned in the previous lecture, much of what we do is not obviously justified by either morality or self-interest. I visit my friend in the hospital; I study philosophy; I bake an elaborate dessert. If the framework in which we conceptualize our reasons and our actions recognizes only self-interested and moral value, then we will have to fit our understanding of these choices into these categories if we are not to regard them as irrational or mistaken. Given the inconvenience and the difficulties involved in these enterprises, however, it is far from clear that they are in my self-interest. Yet to regard them as morally valuable, much less as morally better than any alternatives, is to puff them up in a way that seems both pompous and hard to sustain. Insofar as we feel the need to explain and justify ourselves in terms of these two categories, we will be tempted to distort the character and importance of our interests or to replace them with projects more obviously beneficial to ourselves or more morally admirable.

It might be suggested that the problem here is with thinking that our actions and choices need to be so fully justified. Why can't we sometimes do things just because we want to, without any further justifying reason? We can, but to regard the activities I have I mind as mere arbitrary preferences is also misleading, in a way that sells them short. In fact, I don't perform these acts *just* because I want to. I do want to, but for reasons. I visit my friend because he can use the company, or at least the assurance that his friends care about him (or perhaps I visit him knowing that he is in a coma, just to express my concern for him to myself); I study philosophy because it is interesting and mind-expanding, or, because, in my case, it is part of doing my job well; and I bake because I take pride in my skill as a baker, because I love good food and want to share my enthusiasm for it with others.

Though at least some of these acts have merit that is recognizably moral and are morally preferable to others that might be as good or better for me, and all contribute in some way to my happiness—at the least, I feel the satisfaction of being able to do what I have chosen to do—neither the moral nor the egoistic perspectives capture my perspective in acting, and if we think of such acts only in these terms we will miss the role they play in my or others' lives. I act in these cases not for my sake or the world's; I act neither out of duty nor self-interest. Rather, I am drawn by the particular values of my friend, of philosophy, of a great chocolate cake.[7] These are "objects" whose value has a source outside myself. They would be good, or interesting, or worthwhile whether *I* like or care about or even notice them or not. But they are values I respond to, for which I have an affinity—a subjective attraction, if you will.

Understanding this is important in part because, as I have already said, it enables us to approve of these sorts of interests and activities without distorting the character of their value. It is also important for a proper understanding of self-interest and morality, and of the roles these two types of value and the perspectives they define play and should play in our lives.

Meaning and Self-Interest

One implication that the recognition of meaningfulness as a value has for our concept of self-interest is obvious and familiar. Specifically, if meaningfulness is acknowledged as an ingredient of a good life, and so as an aspect of an enlightened conception of self-interest, and if, as I have argued,

---

[7] For a good recipe, see http://www.epicurious.com/recipes/food/views/chocolate-mousse-cake-with-cinnamon-cream-14010.

meaningfulness cannot be understood as a purely subjective feature of a life, then a hedonistic conception of self-interest, that identifies the best life with a life of maximally good qualitative experience, will not do. An adequate conception of self-interest must include something more than happiness, subjectively construed. Further, we can recognize a paradox of meaningfulness, similar to but deeper than the paradox of hedonism. Because meaning requires us to be open and responsive to values outside ourselves, we cannot be preoccupied with ourselves. If we want to live meaningful lives, we cannot try too hard or focus too much on doing so.

Accepting meaningfulness as an aspect of the good life should also lead us to acknowledge a certain indeterminacy in the concept of self-interest. At least, one will acknowledge this if one thinks, as I do, that meaning is one ingredient of a good life, among others (like subjective happiness). Many things that would contribute to the meaning of a life are difficult, stressful, demanding; they may leave one open to danger or vulnerable to pain. Consider, for example, adopting a child with severe disabilities, or moving to a war-torn country to help its victims find safety or food. Is the more meaningful life better *for oneself* than the one that is easier, safer, more pleasant? There may be no answer to this question. Nor is it obvious that meaning is something it makes sense to want to *maximize* in one's life, even if it does not compete with other self-interested goods.

If the introduction of meaning into one's conception of self-interest makes the latter concept more indeterminate and difficult to apply, it also makes self-interest less significant from a practical perspective. Acknowledging the possibility and desirability of meaning involves accepting the idea that there are values independent of oneself that provide reasons for the activities from which meaning comes.

Though it may not be clear whether the woman whose life has been made more meaningful by the adoption of a child is, all things considered, better off because of it, the woman herself may not care about this. The fact that her relationship with the child adds meaning to her life implies that the relationship engages and, at least partly, fulfills her. Thus, she will have other reasons for being glad to have adopted the child—namely, reasons of love.[8]

Meaning and Morality

The recognition of meaningfulness as a distinct category of value has implications not only for the concept of self-interest, but for our understanding of morality as well. In fact, as with the concept of self-interest, there are implications both for the content of morality and for the role morality can be expected to play in our thoughts and our lives. When thinking about morality, philosophers, if not others, tend to assume that what limits there are to morality are set by the normative and the motivational pull of self-interest. Here perhaps more than anywhere else, a framework that invokes the dichotomy of self-interest and morality tends to be assumed. As we have seen, however, this framework distorts. Relying on it leads us to misunderstand the value of our interests and the actions they motivate us to perform in terms of their contribution to either happiness or moral good, and to cast many of our interests in either a more selfish or a more virtuous light than they deserve.

Curiously, it seems that in practice we do recognize a difference between meaning-enhancing activities and merely

[8] I discuss the relation between meaningfulness and self-interest at greater length in "Happiness and Meaning: Two Aspects of the Good Life," *Social Philosophy & Policy* 14/1 (Winter 1997) 207–225.

self-interested ones in our moral judgments. We give a wider moral berth to people's engagement with the projects or realms from which they get meaning than we do to people's pursuit of happiness, pure and simple. We are less critical of a woman (if critical at all) who misses office hours to go to a philosophy lecture across town than we would be if she were to miss them in order to soak in a hot bath; we are less apt to accuse an amateur musician of decadent expenditure for buying an expensive cello than we would be if he were to spend the same amount on a flat-screen TV. Lying to protect a friend or loved one tends to be regarded as morally quite different (and less blameworthy) than lying to protect oneself. In our theoretical discussion of such judgments, however, the fact that the acts in question do or do not have a role in the meaningfulness of the person's life is frequently obscured. Rather, the value to the agent, or to the world, of the individual's action gets exaggerated, or appeal is made to the questionable idea of a person's duties to herself.

Recognizing explicitly that those activities that sustain the meaningfulness of our lives have a different kind of moral weight than purely self-interested activity is rare in moral theory, but it is not especially problematic. From a moral point of view, we have at least as much reason to want to encourage and increase people's opportunity to live meaningful lives as to live happy ones; we have at least as much reason to recognize the legitimacy of agents' reasons to pursue the realization of values whose source lies outside of the agents themselves as we have to recognize the legitimate pursuit of the agents' own well-being. If the content of our moral principles has not often been framed explicitly to recognize the special place of meaning, there is no obvious reason why it *cannot* be.

The role of meaning in a person's life, and the character of a person's attachment to the things that give her life meaning, however, have implications not only for the content of morality but for its place in our lives, and these implications are more difficult to accommodate. Bernard Williams, one of the few contemporary philosophers to have noticed the distinctive relevance of meaning for morality, has brought this problem vividly to light.

As is well known, Williams criticized both utilitarian and Kantian moralists for failing to appreciate the possibility and nature of a conflict between morality and meaning. In *A Critique of Utilitarianism*, he asks us to consider a man who "is identified with his actions as flowing from projects and attitudes which in some cases he takes seriously at the deepest level, as what his life is about." "It is absurd to demand of such a man," he continues, "when the sums come in from the utility network ... that he should just step aside from his own project and decision and acknowledge the decision which utilitarian calculation requires."[9] In a later essay, Williams goes on to argue that "the Kantian, who can do rather better than [the utilitarian], still cannot do well enough. For impartial morality, if the conflict really does arise, must be required to win; and that cannot necessarily be a reasonable demand on the agent. There can come a point," he writes, "at which it is quite unreasonable for a man to give up, in the name of the impartial good ordering of the world of moral agents, something which is a condition of his having any interest in being around in the world at all."[10]

Though most philosophers have wanted to acknowledge some truth in Williams's criticisms, few have accepted his conclusions. In response to Williams, many have agreed that

[9] J.J.C. Smart and Bernard Williams, *Utilitarianism: For & Against* (Cambridge: Cambridge University Press, 1983) 156.

[10] Bernard Williams, "Persons, Character and Morality," in *Moral Luck* (Cambridge: Cambridge University Press, 1981) 14.

of course morality should take account of the agent's possible sacrifices, weighing them in the balance against the goals and interests of others that morality is concerned to address and protect. Still, most say, there are limits to what a person is morally permitted to do, and if the world conspires to put someone in a position where holding on even to a project "he takes seriously at the deepest level" would require him to cross those limits, morality must stand its ground. After all, they will point out, one man's ground-projects are still *one* man's, and his interests, however fundamental, must be balanced against the interests and rights of others with which their pursuit would interfere.

This response, though not altogether wrong, seems to me to miss the point of Williams's remarks in a way that suggests a failure, on the part of the moralists, to appreciate the difference between self-interest and meaning. One difference, which Williams himself points out, has to do with the special connection meaning has with having a reason to live. What gives meaning to our lives gives us reasons to live, even when we do not care much, for our own sakes, whether we live or die. What gives meaning to our lives gives us reasons to live even when the prospects for our own *well-being* are bleak. Indeed, what gives meaning to our lives may give us reasons beyond that. As Camus pointed out, if something is worth living for, it is also worth dying for.[11] The objects, people, activities, that give meaning to our lives may serve as anchors for our having any interest in the world at all.

Further, we have seen that insofar as our interests and relationships give meaning to our lives, it is because the objects of those interests and relationships have an independent

[11] Albert Camus, *The Myth of Sisyphus and Other Essays* (New York: Alfred A. Knopf, 1955).

value that draws us out of ourselves, linking us to a larger community or world in a positive way. When we act or want to act in the context of these attachments, out of love or passion for their objects, we do not do so purely or primarily for our own sakes (not even, therefore, for the sake of being able to live a meaningful life), but at least partly for the sake of the person or project or value that is the object of our love.

If we keep these features in mind, the moralists' injunction that the agent should sacrifice that which gives meaning to his life for the sake of morality is liable to take on a hollow ring. For first, the suggestion that, hard as it might be, one must sacrifice one's own interests for the sake of the moral order, neglects the possibility that the action one is being asked to take may not present itself under the description of "a sacrifice of one's *own* interests." One's reasons for wanting to take the contrary action are apt rather to be a reflection of one's seeing that action or its goal as independently worthwhile. Second, it is hard to see how reasons for staying within the moral order could override one's reasons for doing something without which one would lose interest in the world, and so presumably in the moral order of the world, altogether.

Ordinarily, people have a number of reasons for wanting to be moral: they have sympathy for others; they want to live on open and equal terms with them; they want to be able to justify their actions to those whom they affect; and, not unimportantly, morality tends to align with self-interest. If, however, being moral would require a person to do something that would deprive him of all interest in the world, it would undermine all these reasons. It is hard to see why nonetheless these reasons should be trumps.

This is not to say that the content of morality should be revised so as to *permit* people to do anything they need to do in order to maintain an interest, if not in their own lives, at least in the world. Williams's concerns may be best understood as making a point, not about the content of morality but about the place it can reasonably be expected to play in a person's life.

Moralists, including the great majority of moral philosophers, tend to assume that morality should occupy an overarching place in one's practical and evaluative outlooks, that it should function unconditionally as a filter through which all a decent person's choices must pass. According to Williams, however, this assumption is unwarranted. To return to the passages I quoted earlier, he thinks that, if it comes down to a conflict between morality and meaning, it is "absurd" or, at any rate, "unreasonable" to demand that morality must win.[12]

Williams himself offers no analysis of meaning, and so the conclusion he leaves us with—namely, that it is not always reasonable to expect a man to be moral—has seemed to many to be either morally subversive or terribly depressing. If I am right, however, about what meaning and our interest in meaning are, we can see his conclusions in a different light.

Meaning, I have argued, comes from active engagement in projects of worth, which links us to our world in a positive way. It allows us to see our lives as having a point and a value even when we take an external perspective on ourselves. It is not clear, however, that the external standpoint from which we ask whether our lives are meaningful need be the same external standpoint as the one from which moral judgments may be thought to issue. Morality, at least as I understand it,

---

[12] The situations of Anna Karenina and of (the fictionalized version of) Gauguin that Williams discusses in the essay "Moral Luck" may be understood as examples of this sort of conflict. See *Moral Luck*, fn 10, above.

is chiefly concerned with integrating into our practical out-
look the fact that we are each one person (or perhaps one
subject) in a community of others equal in status to ourselves. It requires us to act and to restrain our actions in ways
that express respect and concern for others in exchange for
our right to claim the same respect and concern from them.
But there is another perspective, possibly even more external, in which the demands and interests of morality are not
absolute. Viewed from the perspective of our place in the
universe, as opposed to our place in the human or sentient
community, a person's obedience or disobedience to moral
constraints may itself seem to be only one consideration
among others.

A religious view that allows for the possibility that God's
will might diverge from the dictates of human morality is
perhaps the most obvious example of such a perspective. But,
as Nietzsche has shown us, belief in a deity is not necessary in order for it to seem plausible that some values are
independent of and in potential conflict with moral values.
Furthermore, moral values, or morally valuable projects may
themselves conflict. The goodness of one such value or project and the reasons to pursue it may compete with ends and
principles that morality itself demands. From a perspective
that steps back, not just from one's own interests, but from an
absolute commitment to morality itself, if a value or project
with which one's life is bound up (a value or project, in other
words, that gives meaning to one's life) conflicts with a demand of impartial morality, there is, as Williams believes, no
guarantee that the moral demand will win. This perspective,
however, is not egocentric, nor are the values and reasons it
recognizes expressions of selfishness. This has at least two
implications for the way we look at the relation of meaning
to morality and at the possibility of conflict between them.

First, it might make us more ambivalent in our judgment of people who face such conflicts than we would otherwise be. That people should live, and should care about living meaningful lives is, quite generally, a good thing, even if it means that on occasion such people might reasonably be moved to violate moral constraints. When people face a conflict between meaning and morality, we have reason to be sympathetic, and sometimes even to be grateful if they decide not to do what morality requires.

Second, since meaning has an objective (that is, a nonsubjective) component, we do not have to take every individual's claim to face a conflict between meaning and morality at face value. An individual cannot get meaning from worthless projects, much less from projects of wholly negative value. Thus a child-molester cannot get meaning from molesting children, whatever he may think or feel about the matter. The vague proportionality condition on meaning that I mentioned earlier may further limit the kinds of conflict that can plausibly be understood to be ones in which obedience to moral requirements would jeopardize a person's ability to sustain meaning in his life.

Furthermore, the fact that a project's contribution to meaningfulness in a person's life comes in part from her appreciation of the project's independent value may provide a basis for reinterpreting the dilemma in a way that might allow even the person herself to move beyond the impasse the conflict initially appears to present. A woman who gets meaning from her relationship with her daughter might reasonably find the question of whether to break the law to save her daughter's life a difficult one. But not every conflict between morality and the daughter's welfare should be judged to be a difficult choice. Breaking the law to get one's daughter into an elite private school should not be regarded as analogous even if in some sense the woman's relationship with her daughter would be strengthened by the act. The independent, nonsubjective value of the relationship, and of the daughter's good, on which the action's contribution to meaning depends, may be compromised by construing them in a way that insulates them from morality. The meaningfulness of the relationship, if not its strength, might in this case be better preserved by respecting morality rather than by showing oneself willing to give it up.

It cannot be expected that all conflicts between morality and meaning will be resolvable in this way. The possibility that what gives a person's life meaning will come apart from what morality permits will always remain open. This implies that morality is no better suited to serve as an absolute standard for practical reason than self-interest. Still, meaning and an interest in meaning are likely more often than not to complement and reinforce moral concerns. For meaning involves an appreciation of what is valuable independently of one's own interests and attitudes, and an interest in meaning involves an interest in realizing and affirming what is valuable in this way. Moral concerns are perhaps the most obvious and most typically engaging of such valuable aims. Though few people are likely to get meaning in their lives from the abstract project of "being moral"—a passion for morality would be a peculiar and puzzling thing—many if not most people get meaning from more specific projects and relationships that morality should applaud: from being good and doing good in their roles as parent, daughter, lover, friend, and from furthering or trying to further social and political goals.

If we pay increased attention and give increased weight to people's interest in getting and sustaining meaning in their lives, morality and the importance of obedience to its requirements will necessarily occupy a correspondingly smaller place in our practical and evaluational outlooks. But it is arguable that the goals of morality will be as likely or more likely to be achieved, and in a way that is more rewarding to the people who are achieving them, for they will be doing so not out of obedience to duty but out of love.[13]

The Need for the Idea of Objective Value

These last remarks rely not just on the idea of meaningfulness as a category of value in life, but on the particular conception of it that I have urged in these lectures—a conception according to which meaning arises when subjective attraction meets objective attractiveness; that is, a conception according to which meaning comes from active engagement in projects of worth. This conception of meaning manifestly relies on some idea of nonsubjective value, and on the corresponding acceptance of the ideas that some projects, relationships, and activities are better than others, and that the person whose projects and relationships they are may be wrong about their value. These ideas are notoriously controversial and, in secular academic as well as popular culture, we tend to avoid them. The popular Fulfillment View of meaning which I spoke about in the previous lecture, according to which meaning comes from finding and pursuing one's passions, whatever they are, may be understood as implicitly rejecting the idea of objective value, thus conceptualizing meaning in wholly sub-jective terms. The equally popular view that identifies mean-ing with involvement with something "larger than oneself" is opposed to this, but by shying away from any reference to objective value, it deprives itself of the resources neces-sary to answer the challenge, What has size got to do with

---

[13] A related discussion of the relation between meaning and morality is in Susan Wolf, "Meaning and Morality," *Proceedings of the Aristotelian Society* 97 (1997) 299–315.

anything?, or to explain why caring for an infant (presumably smaller than oneself!) can be meaningful while being a groupie for a rock band might not.

Perhaps we avoid talk of objective value out of a desire to stay clear of controversy, perhaps out of fear of being chauvinistic and elitist. Controversy, however, should not be avoided, particularly perhaps in academic and public discourse, and, as I have argued, a belief in the objectivity of values need not be narrow-minded or coercive. One can find the question, *What has objective value?* intelligible and important while remaining properly humble about one's limited ability to discover the answer and properly cautious about the uses to which one's partial and tentative answer may be put. In any event, I have argued that unless we accept the idea of objective value, the concept of meaningfulness, understood to refer to a type of value distinct both from morality and from self-interest, will not be fully intelligible. If we cannot understand what meaningfulness is, our interest in it will diminish and may eventually disappear altogether.

Comments and Response

Comment
John Koethe

I FIND SUSAN WOLF'S ACCOUNT of what makes a
life meaningful persuasive on the whole, and do not intend
to criticize it.[1] What I want to address are some consequences
of a particular application of it. Some may find these consequences troubling, though I myself do not.

On Wolf's account a life is made meaningful by a subjective commitment to, or a love for, a project or activity of
objective worth. The subjective component precludes the
possibility of someone's life being meaningful for reasons
of which she is not cognizant (for example, because it happens to have beneficial effects), which seems implausible.
And the requirement that the project be objectively valuable
precludes a life's being meaningful by virtue of a blind passion for something ridiculous, such as assembling the world's
largest ball of string. There's an ambiguity as to whether calling a project or activity objectively valuable means that it's

[1] I am grateful to Carla Bagnoli, Tom Bamberger, William Bristow, John God-
frey, Edward Hinchman, James Longenbach, Charles North, Susan Stewart, Arthur
Szathmary, and Susan Wolf for discussions and suggestions.

of a *kind* we value (artistic activity, for instance), or whether it means that the project or activity is successfully completed or pursued (say, by actually producing works of artistic value). I'm inclined to think that Wolf means the latter, for she speaks of a scorned artist sustained by the thought that her work is good, and elsewhere she offers the example of a scientist's quest for an important discovery the significance of which is compromised when someone beats him to it.

Having a meaningful life is something we value. One would think then that it ought to be a source of comfort and satisfaction, and that it ought to contribute to one's sense of well-being. Wolf distinguishes between happiness and meaningfulness, between a happy life and a meaningful one. The pursuit of a project of objective value may involve sacrifices and disappointments at odds with living a life that is happy in any conventional sense. But in that case the thought that one's life is a meaningful one, devoted to the pursuit of something objectively worthwhile, would at least seem to offer comfort and consolation.

I imagine that I have been asked to comment on Wolf's lectures both as a poet and as a philosopher, and so I want to consider in particular some possible consequences of her idea of a meaningful life that might apply when the projects involved are certain kinds of aesthetic ones. In an essay on the avant-garde written in the 1960s, the poet John Ashbery remarks that religions are beautiful because of the strong possibility that they're founded on nothing, which he thinks is also true of the kind of art he's discussing. The comparison is apt, though I find the possibility less exhilarating than he does. After modernism, acting on aesthetic impulses of a certain kind involves a "recklessness," as Ashbery puts it, which makes the possibility of failure inherent in or internal to the enterprise itself. I'm not entirely sure how to characterize the kinds of aesthetic impulses and commitments I have in mind, except to say that they are ambitious ones. Of course, like the scientist who's beaten to the discovery to which he's devoted his life, one can always fail in acting on commitments to projects of any sort. But in such a case, it is at least clear what would *count* as success in trying to fulfill the commitment, which is precisely what is *unclear* in the case of the kinds of aesthetic commitments I am talking about.

Let me try to clarify the point by considering a series of examples, starting with Bernard Williams' discussion of Gauguin in his essay on moral luck. Gauguin abandoned his family in Denmark to pursue painting in Paris, an act we may reluctantly excuse on the grounds that (as Wolf might put it) his aesthetic commitments gave him reasons to do what he did additional to his moral reasons to support his family. But as Williams suggests, our verdict would be different if he had turned out to be an untalented hack gripped by a delusion that he was engaged in work of artistic significance, something not precluded by the intensity of his passion for art. The example shows that the meaningfulness of a life depends not just on one's commitments but also on one's success in acting on them. But this, too, is potentially misleading: Gauguin's achievement is so nearly universally recognized that we might suppose success in pursuing aesthetic aims to be typically so clear-cut. Let's consider then three other examples, in which the status of the artistic accomplishment is increasingly problematic.

In *The Banquet Years* Roger Shattuck describes a dinner held in Picasso's studio in 1908 in honor of the painter Henri Rousseau, attended by, among others, Apollinaire, Gertrude and Leo Stein, Marie Laurencin, and Alice Toklas. Rousseau is now regarded as one of modernism's canonical figures, though an anomalous one, but at the time his work was dismissed by art journalists as fraudulent, and the banquet has been interpreted "as a lampooning of Rousseau, as a magnificent farce organized for everyone's enjoyment at [his] expense." Moreover, Rousseau's own assessment of his own and others' work, as when he described himself and Picasso as "the two great painters of this era, you in Egyptian style, I in modern style," seems close enough to delusional to make history's subsequent verdict on his work appear, from the vantage point of 1908, far from inevitable.

Or consider the French poet, novelist, and dramatist Raymond Roussel, whose works describe imaginary tableaux in minute and stupefying detail. His first publication was dismissed as "more or less unintelligible" and "very boring," and while he remains largely unknown, he's had a distinguished list of champions, including the surrealists, André Gide, Jean Cocteau, Marcel Duchamp, Michel Foucault, Alain Robbe-Grillet, and Ashbery. Yet the achievement to which this list testifies falls short of his own assessment of it, for he claimed to his psychiatrist Pierre Janet that he was the equal of Dante and Shakespeare, and that he had to close the curtains of his room when he wrote, lest the intense light emanating from his pen endanger the world outside.

Consider finally the "outsider" artist Henry Darger, a reclusive Chicago janitor who gained prominence when an epic narrative of over fifteen thousand pages, *The Story of the Vivian Girls, in What Is Known as the Realms of the Unreal*, profusely illustrated with hundreds of watercolors and drawings, was discovered after his death in 1973. His work, the paintings and drawings in particular, has had considerable cultural effect, inspiring, for example, a book-length poem, *Girls on the Run*, by (who else?) Ashbery. And while Darger's work is undeniably powerful, simultaneously innocent and sinister, with vibrant coloration and complex compositional qualities, it is also unsettling in ways that have little to do with aesthetics: it can be extremely violent, and the girls are often depicted with male genitalia, quite possibly because Darger didn't know any better; and it is unclear whether what one sees in looking at it is the fulfillment of an aesthetic commitment or the manifestation of a disturbing psychological compulsion. Probably the right thing to say is that it is simply indeterminate which it is.

These are extreme examples, and the three artists described seem oblivious to the possibility that they might be affected by delusions. But they are meant to suggest something that is true of more typical cases as well: namely, that it is difficult to distinguish, from the vantage point of the artist, between the successful achievement of serious aesthetic aims and the delusion that one has them and that they've been achieved; and this difficulty complicates the question of whether one's life is meaningful or wasted. One has to work, as it were, in the shadow of an awareness of the latter possibility. One can of course always be mistaken in thinking that one has fulfilled commitments one has undertaken, whatever their nature. What's distinctive about the kinds of aesthetic aims I'm talking about is that the possibility of delusion is internal to them, and that by their very nature, clear criteria for success in fulfilling them are lacking. Stanley Cavell makes a similar point in "Music Discomposed," when he suggests "that the possibility of fraudulence, and the experience of fraudulence, is endemic in the experience of contemporary music," a possibility he takes to be inherent in the very nature of the kinds of musical compositions he's discussing. I think Cavell is responding to the popular suspicion of the 1940s and 50s as to whether avant-garde music, painting, and so on were really art at all ("Why, my kid could do that if she'd just stop drawing Thanksgiving turkeys and stoop to it!"), which in retrospect seems quaint.

Of course they're art. But the question remains whether in any given case the art is of significance or importance.

None of this is meant to suggest that aesthetic value isn't objective, or at least as objective as Wolf takes it to be. The judgments others make of my work or I make of others' work can be objectively correct, and they need not be subject to the inherent possibility of self-deception or delusion I'm talking about. The possibility I have in mind seems viewpoint-dependent (as Cavell's worry about fraudulence doesn't), one that appears from my first-person perspective as an artist, and that neither the phenomenological character of my subjective commitments nor the assurances of others suffice to dispel—since the former could be the same whether or not the work succeeds, and (quite apart from *banquet Rousseau*-like worries) a too ready acceptance of my work by others could well be a sign that it has failed. Something comparable occurs in arguments for philosophical skepticism, where a crucial premise is my inability to rule out some outlandish hypothesis like, for instance, that I'm a brain in a vat. *You* know perfectly well that I'm not, but the problem is how *I* could know this. Ordinarily, if you know something and inform me of it, I can thereby come to know it, too. But this doesn't work in the case of skepticism, and it doesn't work in the artistic case either. I don't want to press this comparison too far though, or treat the possibility of aesthetic delusion as merely a special instance of a general skeptical worry, for while it is perfectly alright for me to ignore the skeptical possibilities as ridiculous (even if I cannot rule them out in a principled manner), it is part of the nature of artistic endeavor that I cannot dismiss the possibility of delusion or self-deception out of hand.

How disturbing is this? Even if it jeopardizes my ability to derive satisfaction and comfort from a life based on aesthetic commitments, and of appealing to the non-moral reasons that flow from them, I do not myself think that it is cause for much concern—it is simply a predicament I have to live with. ("For us, there is only the trying. The rest is not our business." T. S. Eliot, "Burnt Norton") But if the reader finds it unsettling, there are several possible ways to handle the problem within Wolf's framework. One is to take the criterion of success in fulfilling aesthetic ambitions to be a readily recognized competence. A second is to take it to be acceptance by a suitably constituted community. And a third is to take it to be helping maintain the artistic enterprise you are engaged in, whatever the ultimate importance of your own work. (" . . . one who marched along with, 'made common cause,' yet had neither the gumption nor the desire to trick the thing into happening." Ashbery, "Sortes Vergilianae"). I don't find the first two strategies appealing, and the third is hard to spell out, but for reasons of time I will not explore them here. I will close instead with an illustrative anecdote. In 1968 I was driving across the country and stopped in Iowa City to see Ted Berrigan, who had just begun a year of teaching at the Iowa Writers' Workshop. In those days there really *was* a distinction, as I don't think there is anymore, between academic and nonacademic poetry, and it seemed odd to think of Berrigan, the presiding figure of the quintessentially nonacademic second generation of New York School poets, teaching at what many considered, perhaps unfairly, a main training ground for academic poetry. Naturally I wanted to know what he thought of his students, and he said they were fine, except that they all wanted to be minor poets, which he took to betray a crippling lack of ambition. It is ironic then that that's what Berrigan, who died in 1983, is—a minor poet, something I mean as high praise. Major poets are such because of the range and depth of their accomplishment and influence, but to be an enduring minor poet—as opposed to just a representative figure of a certain period and milieu—is a tremendous achievement. All the same, I'm not sure how much satisfaction Berrigan would have taken in it.

Comment
Robert M. Adams

PEOPLE SPEAK OFTEN ENOUGH of a human life as being meaningful or meaningless, having or lacking a meaning, either at a given time or in its history as a whole. Almost always, when we think in those terms, we want to find meaning in our lives; we do not want them to be meaningless. Philosophers, at least in the English-speaking world, have published relatively little about meaningfulness in life, despite its apparently profound human importance. We have found the concept of it a tough nut to crack and pry open.

A most welcome exception to this generalization is Susan Wolf's account of "meaning in life." In her view, "meaning arises from loving objects worthy of love and engaging with them in a positive way." That seems to me insightful and right-headed. It also seems fruitful, offering a way forward in thinking about this difficult topic.

Wolf conceives of meaningfulness of life as having both a subjective and an objective side. It has a subjective side insofar as it involves love and positive engagement, and an objective side insofar as what one loves in a meaningful way must be worthy of love, must have value independent of oneself.

A further interesting and important structural feature of Wolf's thinking is her insistence that meaningfulness offers a perspective on the evaluation of lives that is distinct from those of self-interest and morality. A meaningful life is not the same as a happy life or a morally good life.

I

The questions I want to pursue first have to do mainly with the subjective side of Wolf's view. In particular, it is not clear to me why she should *not* say that the *only* requirement, on the subjective side, for meaning in life is love, and acting coherently for reasons of love. Why add any requirement of feelings of fulfillment?

One sort of fulfillment that *could* be part of a life's meaning is the success of one's major projects, insofar as that is the fulfillment of those purposes in which one's love is expressed. It is plausible to think that it could make a difference to the meaning of your life whether you succeed in a major project—for instance, whether you finish your big book before you die. Not that the incompleteness or failure of your project necessarily deprives the project—let alone your whole life—of meaning. We may well believe that "it's better to have loved and lost than never to have loved at all." Still, it seems reasonable to think that the meaning of one's life might be *enhanced* by the completion of a big book. And *what* an intellectual's life means can surely be affected by what actually got written and what actually got published.

Though success and failure can make a difference to a life's meaning, I believe that a life can derive meaning of the greatest value from a project that has failed. The archetypal case of such meaning-laden failure, in our cultural tradition, is the projects of Jesus that failed in his crucifixion. A probably related case that connects interestingly with our topic is

Claus von Stauffenberg's project of rescuing Germany from Nazism, which culminated in his attempt to assassinate Hitler and lead a coup d'état, on July 20, 1944. His project failed and cost some hundreds of deaths, including his own. Yet his life, especially in its last year or so, seems extremely meaningful to most of those who know about it—and rightly so, in my opinion.

Did Stauffenberg himself, in the end, find his life meaningful because of his project, despite its failure? From what I have read about him it seems practically certain that he did. But suppose he did not. More precisely, suppose that in the moment of failure he was so disappointed and so depressed that he thought his life was meaningless. Should we in that case conclude that it was in fact meaningless? I think that conclusion would be very implausible.

I raise this question because Wolf contends that if one's involvement with "something larger than oneself" does not bring the "reward" of *finding* the involvement meaningful, then "it is unclear that it contributes to meaning in one's life at all." If this means that one's life is not meaningful unless one sees it as meaningful when one looks back upon it, then I would disagree. Of course, the view backwards is not the only view by which one might assess the meaningfulness of one's life. If I love in such a way that purposes springing from my love make sense to me, and I act on those purposes and they seem to me worth acting on, then to that extent I think I may find my life meaningful *in* living it, regardless of how it may look in retrospect. I am inclined to agree that love does not confer meaning on one's life unless it gives rise to purposes that make sense to one in that way. And I take it that this is part of what Wolf has in mind.

I'm not persuaded, however, that consciousness of meaning, or valuing one's life, either retrospectively or while acting, need involve *feeling good*. Not much is known about how Stauffenberg *felt* when he was finally compelled to recognize, late in the evening of July 20th, that his conspiracy to overthrow Nazism had failed. Someone he spoke to then thought he looked "indescribably sad."[1] Great sadness would certainly have been appropriate to the context. It does not follow that it would not also have been appropriate for him to see his life, and his efforts to rescue his country from Nazism, as meaningful.

Attitudes and feelings can be complex. It would be possible for Stauffenberg, in the hour of recognizing the failure of his project, to feel awful about the fate he foresaw for Germany, and at the same time to find some consolation in the thought, "At least I don't have to despise myself. I've done what I could." But consolation is different from fulfillment, and it need not involve feeling good on the whole. This is terribly important. For one of the great things about positive meaning in life is that one can have it even when one's hopes and projects are not fulfilled and one does not feel good.

I grant that *some* of one's feelings can affect, or enter into, the meaning of one's life. In a meaning-constituting love, what one feels pleased about, and what one feels sad about, should cohere with one's commitments. The meaning of the feelings in those cases rides on their intentionality; it's a matter of what one feels good or bad *about*. But feeling good or feeling bad does not necessarily have any intentional content. One can feel "up" or feel depressed without those feelings being clearly *about* anything. And it seems very doubtful that

[1] Peter Hoffman, *Stauffenberg: A Family History, 1905–1944* (Cambridge University Press, 1995) 276, summarizing the report of Delia Ziegler, a secretary who worked in the same office as Stauffenberg.

feelings, good or bad, without intentional content enter into the meaning or meaninglessness of one's life.

II

This is a point at which it seems to me that there is an important analogy between meaning in life and other sorts of meaning, such as the meanings of words, the meanings of texts, what we mean to say, and what we mean to do. Wolf does not raise these questions, and it could be that she is wise not to raise them. Words can have different meanings that do not illuminate each other in any very interesting way, and this could be true of the word "meaning" itself. Wolf's account provides an illuminating explication of a way in which people surely do speak of lives having "meaning," whether or not there is an enlightening analogy between it and other meanings of "meaning." In fact, however, I believe there are similarities worth noticing.

One has to do with intentionality. What you *mean* is what you intend. To say you *mean* to do something is to say you *intend* to do it. To say that in saying, "He's very cool" in a certain context you *meant* that the person in question is attractively stylish, is to say that you *intended* to express that sort of approval. In a more general semantic view, what our language means depends on how it is related to what it is about. We speak of such cognitive content, perhaps metaphorically, as a matter of intentionality, of what the language stretches out to grasp, which we call its "intentional object."

It is worth trying on the hypothesis that meaning in life, on its subjective side, is a matter of intentionality. This hypothesis fits Wolf's view at important points. Love is certainly an intentional attitude. Similarly, Wolf speaks of fulfillment having "a cognitive component," which even the "deep and intense pleasure" of "eating a perfectly ripe peach" does not have. What I take it she thinks the pleasure of eating lacks, is the intentional content it would have if it were in part a regarding of something as objectively good.

A second point at which there may be an analogy between the meaning of a life and the meaning of a linguistic utterance concerns *communication*. Both about someone's verbal statement and about someone's life, one can ask what it means *to other people*. What a life means to the person who lives it, in her understanding of it, belongs presumably to the subjective side of our topic. What her life means or communicates to other people should be seen perhaps as belonging to a third side of the topic, *intersubjective* rather than purely objective. This can be a very important aspect of a life's meaning. Claus von Stauffenberg provides an example here too. He and his co-conspirators seem to have been motivated in large part by the meaning they hoped their deeds would have for others, believing that even if it couldn't succeed in its own terms, the plot against Hitler should be attempted for the honor of Germany, to show the world that some Germans stood up against Hitler's crimes.[2]

A third analogy has to do with *rational* or *intelligible structure*. The meaning of a linguistic utterance or text depends heavily on various aspects of its structure. There is no sharp line between rational or structural incoherence and meaninglessness. Something similar appears to be true about meaning in one's life, which seems to be undermined if one's major purposes do not cohere with each other, or do not remain stable over at least a significant period of time, or are not expressed in one's actions. I think this will be pretty widely agreed.

[2] *Stauffenberg*, 238. 243.

Less easily granted, perhaps, but worth taking seriously, in my opinion, is the idea that those things that happen to people through no choice of their own can enter in a structural way into the meaning or meaninglessness of their lives. To take an example again from the Second World War: Heinrich Böll's *And Where Were You, Adam?*[3] about the last stages of the war on the eastern front, may be seen as portraying the lives and deaths of retreating German soldiers as meaningless. In speaking of meaninglessness here I am I think responding mainly to the story's description of arbitrariness and a lack of coherent purpose in the commands and actions to which those soldiers were subjected by the collapsing German war machine. I find it a plausible representation of an all too possible sort of meaninglessness in life, in which the ordinary soldiers were certainly complicit, but of which most of them were definitely not the primary authors. No doubt such meaninglessness in an individual's life depends also on not having coherent purposes of one's own to act on. But it can be very difficult, and for many impossible, to organize one's own life around coherent purposes if one's social context lacks coherent meaning. If our lives have meaning, we do not create it all by ourselves.

III

I want finally to say something about the *objective* side of Wolf's account. I will leave aside questions, which could be raised, about whether a life (Hitler's, for example) could be meaningful but with a meaning that is objectively bad rather than good. I want to focus on Wolf's claim that the objective perspective that is crucial for the meaning of a life is distinct

---

[3] Translated by Leila Vennewitz (London: Secker and Warburg, 1974).

from that of impartial morality, though not unrelated to it. I want to underline both a difficulty we may feel in accepting this claim, and the very important appeal I think we should nonetheless find in it.

Stauffenberg is again a case in point. I certainly believe (and imagine Wolf would agree) that his actions against Nazism could be *justified* from a perspective of impartial morality. The difference to which Wolf calls attention begins to bite when we ask whether his actions were actually done with the *intention* of satisfying principles and concerns that are impartially other-regarding. It bites even deeper when we ask whether those actions were driven by impartially other-regarding *motives*. What was Stauffenberg's central motive, the love at the heart of his project? Most of what I have read about him suggests that it was *patriotism*, his love for Germany, rather than an impartial love for humanity in general.

Not that his patriotism was amoral. Fundamental in his motivation was his loathing of Nazi crimes;[4] but he viewed the moral wrongness of those crimes through the lens of patriotism. He saw them as a disgrace to Germany, which demanded a German response. Moreover, he wished to extricate Germany not only from crimes against humanity but also from the Nazis' war, which he, like most of the German military leadership, saw as heading toward a catastrophic national defeat. These are not *impartially* other-regarding motives. But it does not follow that what is loved in them is *not* an objective good of the sort that is at the center of Wolf's account of the objective side of meaning in life.

Patriotism is a morally dangerous love, which has inspired enormous wrongs and follies. Can love of country really

---

[4]Including persecution of the Jews, and crimes against Poles and other Eastern Europeans. See, for example, *Stauffenberg*, xiv–xv, 226, 283.

have an object good enough to satisfy Wolf's criterion on the objective side? In part it surely can, for patriotism typically springs in large part from caring about one's family and friends and the other people among whom one has lived, and about the goods of the culture in which one has been educated. There is much of objective, positive value in that. And when we consider also the ethical dimension of Stauffenberg's patriotism manifest in his shame about Nazi crimes, it is hard to deny that his patriotism had positive value of a kind that can sustain objective meaning in life.

We may still feel some moral unease about Stauffenberg's patriotism. It inspired not only his conspiracy against Hitler, but also his service in military aggressions launched by the Nazi government. If we went into the details of what he wanted for his country, I suspect that most of us would be at best ambivalent about some of his goals. (Probably, of course, we should also be at best ambivalent about some things in our own lives.) Stauffenberg himself was hardly without ambivalence toward his moral record. His conception of a military officer's responsibility did not allow him to acquit himself of the guilt of crimes committed by German officials acting supposedly for Germany. It appears that he and other conspirators were motivated in part by a feeling of guilt "that they had been too slow to oppose the evil."[5]

The place of guilt in this story points to an important difference between meaning in life and virtue. I take judgments of virtue (or vice) to be assessments of a person's character at a given time. Virtue and vice as such do not have a narrative structure, though narratives may reveal virtue or vice. But judgments of meaning in life are assessments of something that does have a narrative structure. And a life-narrative that

---

[5] *Stauffenberg*, xiv.

has very positive meaning as a whole can include things that are negatively valued. For instance, it can include guilt, as part of a narrative structure of guilt and expiation.

Stauffenberg's patriotism was at any rate not a form of *impartial* moral virtue. But that should not distract us from the decisive point in assessing the meaning of his life objectively, which is (in my opinion) his extraordinary response to the objective values that were salient in his situation in the last months of his life. In an appalling context that demoralized to some extent most who worked within it, Stauffenberg could see a path that held at least a slight hope of leading to a better future for his country—a future better in moral as well as other respects than the future toward which it was heading. And his patriotism inspired him to follow that path, not only with courage, but with an energy, tenacity, and resourcefulness more or less unique among the rather many German officers who recognized at least implicitly what needed to be done. I find that awesomely meaningful. And shame on me if I fancy myself in a position to look down on Stauffenberg! In such a context it seems particularly important to be able to recognize, as Wolf urges, a very important kind of positive meaningfulness in a life that responds to objective goods with motives of love that are not impartially moral motives.

Comment
Nomy Arpaly

I WOULD LIKE TO APPLAUD Susan Wolf for standing in front of an interdisciplinary crowd and declaring: *I am conducting research with no practical implications that I know of, and I am proud.* Philosophy, even the philosophy of human values—and for that matter the search after knowledge and understanding in general—needs practical justification like a fish needs a bicycle. In fact, of the various things that tell us apart from other apes, the ability and inclination to pursue nonpractical interests is one of the truly priceless.

Which leads us to another thing for which I would like to thank Wolf. I would like to thank her for simply reminding us that our motives are not restricted to the usual twin suspects—self interest and moral duty, and that situations in which we act from neither are not rare. There are other things that people care about for their own sake, ranging from Truth and Beauty to the New England Patriots. One might think that this point is a simple one, but that would be to overlook the significant fact that so many of us still write as if this simple point had never occurred to us—perhaps taking a cue from Kant and his drama of duty and inclination. The oversight is particularly amazing to me because while acting for non-moral, unselfish reasons is common to all humans, we philosophers are among those most often subjected to the question, "Why on earth do you do this?" Even among ourselves we do not escape such inquiries. In a forgetful moment, with a lamentable lack of empathy, a philosopher who writes about the paradoxes of time travel will dare to wonder aloud why her colleague is interested in so obscure a topic as demonstratives. The "why" question posed to us (as well as to oologists, for example) by more conventional segments of the workforce is a constant reminder of "the things we do for love." "We" here means "everyone," and the locution is borrowed from the characters of *A Chorus Line*, who themselves are pondering their motives for pursuing the lives of poor actors.

What I would like to question is the necessary role Wolf claims objective worth has in providing meaning in life. Suppose one takes a fulfillment view along the following lines: one has a meaningful life if the ten things she cares most about and the things she does all the time are related in a certain good way, whereas one is up for a midlife crisis if the ten things she cares about most and the things she does all the time have nothing to do with each other. To that, Wolf adds a constraint: those ten things (or however many there are) should have a modicum of objective worth. She appeals to our intuitions with her goldfish case: if what I care about most is my goldfish, and what gives me fulfillment is simply caring for my goldfish, then regardless of that fulfillment I still lead a meaningless life. Devotion to something that is not worthwhile cannot give meaning to my life. I do not wish to *attack* this claim but merely to point out ways in which the fulfillment theorist might be able to account for "goldfish" cases, and to explain why we look with pity at the goldfish monomaniac's life without either dismissing our pity or appealing to some objective value that is missing from the theorist's picture.

I will make the following claim about the normal adult human who receives full satisfaction in her life from keeping a goldfish: she does not exist. There is no such person. No doubt there exists at least one person who claims, believes, and even feels that her goldfish and only her goldfish makes her life meaningful. After all, the goldfish case is not so far removed from the cases of many actual people who credit all the meaning in their lives to some delightful dog or elegant cat, at times making assertions about the importance of the furry creature in making their lives meaningful that would sound exaggerated even if they were talking about, say, adult offspring. If you don't believe me, visit www.marryyourpet. com, where you and your pet are invited to tie the knot if you, like many other humans, realize that your relationship with your pet gives you much more than any human partner can. The decor of the page is hearts and flowers, and the testimonials from happy couples are full of passion: they might once have had trouble finding fulfillment in their lives, but that was *before* they found their dog . . . .

But if we were to meet Wolf's Goldfish Nut and her real life counterparts we would not believe their testimonials, even if we were otherwise quite inclined to believe what people say about themselves. Why is this? The first answer that leaps off the Web page is: because they are deluded. Never mind absolute values: they are deluded about facts. That is, they say things like, "Hey look, my goldfish knows when I am talking about him," or "Nobody understands me except my cat." These claims contradict what we know about the brains of cats and fish. The delusion can go further: people who marry their pets, for example, must think of them as capable of meaningfully saying "yes" to a marriage proposal and of respecting a human ceremony. This is, again, a rather straightforward misrepresentation of dogs and cats—and an even greater misrepresentation of goldfish. Even if the Goldfish Nut makes no such openly deluded statement, we suspect a misrepresentation somewhere. Why? Because the Goldfish Nut's life appears to be one in which some basic human needs are not being met, where things that we know are necessary for fulfillment are absent. For example, how likely is it that any human other than a severely autistic one could be fulfilled absent intimate relationships with other humans—whether of friendship, romantic love, sexual attraction, parenthood, identification with a group, or small everyday intimacies, such as those of play? Consider too that much of Goldfish Nut's brain remains unused. She does not experience the satisfaction of learning or even of gradually becoming better at a task, or the satisfaction of doing something that is appreciated by other humans or that merits taking pride in her skill. Basic emotional needs, even very general and disjunctive ones, remain unsatisfied for her. If she still says that she is fulfilled, we wonder, is she perhaps severely depressed, no longer remembering what fulfillment feels like? Did she get too burnt when her last project or relationship failed, so that she wants to believe, self-deceptively, that she can do well without attempting anything in the least challenging? Does staring at her goldfish constitute some kind of Buddhist experiment or art project that she won't tell us about? The alternative—to simply accept her claim that she is fulfilled and satisfied—means seeing her as so immensely removed from our experience of healthy adult humans that we might need a global revision of what we believe about our species.

We could, of course, try and imagine a case in which a life based on caring for a goldfish would not have these grim implications. Take a retarded child, living in an institution,

who suddenly develops a fascination with goldfish after seeing them on TV. With help, and with immense effort on his
own part, he manages to learn how to keep his own goldfish,
and this achievement puts a spring in his step. The staff, comparing him to his peers who do nothing but doze in front of
the TV, might wish that the others might find such meaningful projects for themselves. They might find the child's interest in the fish heartwarming, and they would not be wrong.
Goldfish care can give a retarded child fulfillment, because
it gives him what it cannot give an adult. In caring for the
fish, the child, unlike the adult, may well be working at the
edge of his abilities, giving himself challenges and reasons to
feel pride. The arrival of the fish in his life probably results
in *more* interactions with other humans rather than fewer
(children and others come to see the pretty fish, rapport is
achieved with the adults who help) and more expressions of
social approval come his way. Knowing how to do something
on his own gives him a sense of self-efficacy. In short, being
in charge of a beloved goldfish or two can give the retarded
child a measure of fulfillment that would require much bigger projects in a normal adult—but for the same reasons and
via the same mechanisms. Thus, in the case of the child it is
not strange to say that goldfish keeping gives his life meaning. Both the implausibility of the meaningful adult goldfish-
based life and the plausibility of a retarded child's meaningful
(fairly) goldfish-based life can both be explained without appealing to any objective value (or disvalue) that fish-raising
might have, but simply by citing intuitions and the occasional
empirical study on what makes humans fulfilled.

Let us move to a second point. Wolf presents "meaning"
as a value and a motive—a third party to the usual suspects,
duty and self-interest. As examples of people who act from
considerations of meaning, she suggests people who act from

parental love, from aesthetic ideals (the perfect pastry), and from love of any number of possible people and objects. Here she is surely mistaken. Those who act, say, for the love of art, do not act for the sake of a meaningful life but rather for the sake of art. Their reason for action is not "doing so will make my life more meaningful," but rather "doing so will help art." If I love the Basque language, I believe that the Basque language is valuable for its own sake, whether or not it contributes meaning to the life of the individual that is me (whether or not, in fact, I exist). Bernard Williams convinced many of us that if you are faced with a situation in which you can help either your wife or a stranger, and you think, "I am going to help my wife because she is my wife and in such conditions it is morally permissible to prefer your wife," then you have thought one thought too many. But imagine a person who thinks, "I am going to help my wife because she is my wife and love for my wife is among the things that make my life meaningful." That, too, is one thought too many. It may not be egotistical, but it is inappropriately agent-centered. So read properly, Wolf's position does not introduce a "third party" value—that of meaning in life—but rather asserts the legitimacy of many, many values that people might hold: each wife or husband truly loved presents their spouse with a value consideration independent of any other, including "meaning." I see no problem here for Wolf, except that if she wishes to make claims specifically about meaningfulness as a value, she needs to keep clear the distinction and relation between that and one's wife as a value or one's art as a value.

But does she want to? I would like to end with a question—maybe a few questions. In her previous writing, Wolf has stated that it is wrong to expect a neat hierarchy of values with morality on top. I understood her to be saying that the same would be true of a hierarchy of values with prudence on top, or truth, or beauty, or even a "healthy balance" or *eudaimonia*. There is no top. From the point of view of morality, one must always be moral, from the point of view of prudence one must always do the prudent thing, and much the same is true of any value. When deciding between two values, we are "on our own"—that is, there exists no argument that can, independently of the point of view embodied by each value, tell us which of the choices would be right for us. It appears that Wolf has changed her mind over the years, though she still opposes the idea of a hierarchy and a "top," and still takes it that in some cases we are on our own when choosing between values. She can now say, for example, that pursuing your love of art is a great idea *unless it entails extreme immorality*. It is as if there may be a top, but instead of commanding our every deliberative move it is restricted to issuing such commandments as, "Let's not get carried away!" I would like to ask Wolf how she sees the relationships between the plethora of values that she is talking about. Is there a top? If there is not, where do "within reason"-type statements come from? How much can we say about relationships between values? Should the notion of particularism come to mind? Or perhaps the idea of incomparable or incommensurable choices? What does it take for there to be—even sometimes—a truth as to which love I should follow when my loves conflict, a truth that is both independent of my own concerns and strongest inclinations? Could it be that morality does have some kind of privileged status among values, after all? It may be that I am posing too many questions here, that what I really want is not so much immediate and specific answers as a sequel. Not that I understand why anyone would want to do metaethics, anyway!

Comment
Jonathan Haidt

Finding Meaning in Vital Engagement and Good Hives

AT THE AGE OF FIFTEEN I began calling myself an atheist. It was bad timing because the next year, in English class, I read *Waiting for Godot* and plunged into a philosophical depression. This was not a clinical depression with thoughts of personal worthlessness and a yearning for death. It was, rather, the kind of funk that Woody Allen's characters so often exhibited in his early movies. For example, in *Annie Hall*, a flashback shows us a nine-year-old Allen-esque boy being asked by a doctor why he is depressed. The boy's response is that he has recently learned that the universe will expand forever and someday break apart. He sees no further point in doing homework, despite his mother's protestations that Brooklyn is not expanding.

After reading *Godot*, I felt the same way. If there was no God then my life, and all life, suddenly seemed to be as pointless as the lives of Vladimir and Estragon. Here, for example, is the quote I chose later that year to place under my picture in my high school yearbook: "*Whosoever shall not fall by the sword or by famine, shall fall by pestilence, so why bother shaving?*" The quote is from Woody Allen.[1]

The next year I went to college. I was committed to figuring out the meaning of life, and I thought that studying philosophy would help. I was disappointed. Philosophy addressed many fundamental questions of being and knowing, but the question "What is the meaning of life?" never came up. I assumed it was a badly formed question, and I moved on. I went to graduate school in psychology. If only I had been able to read Susan Wolf back then! She clarifies the question so elegantly, and she points to the means by which each of us can answer it for ourselves: go find something to love, something *worthy* of love, that you can link to and engage with in the right sort of way.

It took me a while to do that, but I eventually did, as so many of us have, both by committing to people and by committing to my work. My remaining comments flow from that work, which ended up bringing me, by a roundabout route, back to the question of the meaning of life. A few years ago I wrote a book that reviewed ten of the greatest psychological ideas of all time, from the vantage point of modern science.[2] The last chapter was on happiness and the meaning of life. In writing that chapter I came across two extraordinarily powerful ideas. The first idea is *vital engagement*, the second one is *hive psychology*. I will suggest that these two concepts, taken together, can help solve the problem of objective meaning that Wolf raised in these lectures.

---

[1] Woody Allen, *Without Feathers* (New York: Random House, 1975).

[2] Jonathan Haidt, *The Happiness Hypothesis: Finding Modern Truth in Ancient Wisdom* (New York: Basic Books, 2006).

Vital Engagement

Some people live extraordinarily generative lives. They design, write, build, nurture, cure, discover, or invent. They contribute to the knowledge or well-being of humanity to such a degree that others are motivated to give them awards or to write books about them. Most of these people are happy, and nearly all are passionately engaged in their work. Many of us want to know, how did they get that way? And how can *I* get some of that?

The psychologist Mihaly Csikszentmihalyi interviewed over a hundred such eminent people to find out. He and his students have given us a picture of a way of living that they call "vital engagement," which they define as "a relationship to the world that is characterized both by experiences of flow (enjoyed absorption) and by meaning (subjective significance)."[3] Flow is the psychological state that results when you are completely immersed in an activity that is challenging, yet closely matched to your abilities. You can achieve it while painting, dancing, writing, driving on a winding road, or playing video games. Flow is not meaning, but it is a kind of deep interest. Extraordinarily productive people usually began their careers with deep interest—they were drawn to an activity, and often found at least brief moments of flow in that activity. But then, gradually, over many years, vital engagement emerged as the person wove an ever more encompassing web of knowledge, action, identity, and relationships.

Here is an example. When I first taught a class on positive psychology I was trying to explain the concept of vital

[3] Jeanne Nakamura and Mihaly Csikszentmihalyi, "The Construction of Meaning through Vital Engagement," in *Flourishing: Positive Psychology and the Life Well-Lived*, eds. C.L.M. Keyes and J. Haidt (Washington D.C.: American Psychological Association, 2003) 83–104; the quote is on p. 87.

engagement, and the class wasn't getting it. I suspected that we had an example in our midst, a shy woman who had said little so far, but who had revealed that she was passionate about horses. I asked her to tell us how she got involved in riding. She spoke of her childhood love of animals, and of how she had begged her parents to let her take riding lessons. She rode for fun at first, but soon began entering competitions. Riding became ever more important to her, and she chose to attend the University of Virginia because of its excellent riding team.

After telling us these basic facts, she stopped talking, unsure of how much I wanted her to say. I wanted more, because vital engagement is not just doing and loving. I wanted to know if she had been gradually engulfed in a web of horse-related meanings. I asked her if she could name specific horses from previous centuries. She said yes, she had begun to study the history of horses as soon as she began to ride. I asked her if she had made friends through riding, and she told us that most of her close friends were "horse friends." This woman was a perfect exemplar of vital engagement. She had a relationship to riding that had begun with simple interest and had expanded over many years to tie her into an activity, a tradition, and a community. This woman had found more than happiness; she had found meaning.

I tell this story because I want to agree with Wolf's emphasis on the *quality* of connection. My favorite statement of her Fitting Fulfillment theory is this one: *"Meaning... comes from active engagement in projects of worth, which links us to our world in a positive way."* By speaking about "active engagement" and about linking to the world in a positive way, I think she is advocating something close to the notion of vital engagement. But in her claim that the project must be "of worth" she has committed herself to a search for objective value. In fact, she ends her essay with the claim that without a concept of objective value, the concept of meaningfulness (as a type of value distinct from both morality and self-interest) will not be fully intelligible.

This creates a difficulty. Wolf bets everything on the existence, or at least intelligibility, of objective value. I would bet against her. I do not think there can be such a thing as objective value in the form that she and many other philosophers hope to find. Wolf herself is aware of the challenges. She asserts that a meaning-giving project must provide value to someone other than the self, but she recognizes that "independent value" is not enough. If two people find meaning by providing value to each other, how is this any better than two people earning a living by taking in each others' laundry? She also raises the danger of elitism, the problem of "who is to say" from an external perspective that an activity is a worthwhile or fitting one. I think that this problem, too, is insoluble. Note the kinds of activities Wolf thinks are likely to be objectively worthwhile: being engaged with political and social causes, creating art, preserving natural beauty, developing one's potential. She admits that these presuppose bourgeois American values, but I think they are even narrower; they presuppose *politically liberal* bourgeois American values.

But *does Wolf really need a theory of objective value?* I suspect that she fears that if there is no such thing as objective value, then meaning-relativism will prevail, and lawn mower racing, flagpole sitting, and rock rolling will have just as strong a claim to being meaningful as writing a symphony or righting an injustice. Here is where vital engagement comes to the rescue. *Lawn mower racing and flagpole sitting do not lend themselves to vital engagement.* People do such things for fun, and to get into record books. They might even find friendship along the way. But how many of them found flow in these activities as adolescents, devoured all the books they could find on the history of lawn mowers and flagpoles, lovingly assembled collections of lawn mowers and flagpoles, and chose colleges and jobs so as to ensure that they would always be able to race mowers or sit on poles in the company of other mower racers and pole sitters?

What is more, if Professor Wolf sticks to her quest for objective value, I fear she must tell my former student that her love of horses is in danger of being declared meaningless, if someone ever does come up with an adequate theory of objective value. After all, all of her horsing around does nothing for anyone else, and it does not make the world a better place. My student may feel vitally engaged, but the joy she gets from riding horses around in circles might just make of her another Sisyphus fulfilled.

Hive Psychology

The second psychological idea that I think might help Wolf develop her argument is hive psychology.[4] We in the social sciences have been plagued by a sixty-year-long attack of methodological individualism. Most of us are firmly committed to a Newtonian approach that aims at producing the simplest possible model and then builds complexity into that model only when it is absolutely necessary. We think about society as a set of billiard balls bouncing around, each with its own magnetic attractions and repulsions. I think philosophy is just as deeply infected, and I see billiard balls bouncing around in some parts of Wolf's essay. Note this passage:

> I am *drawn* by the particular values of my friend, of philosophy, of a great chocolate cake. These are "*objects*" whose value

[4] For a review, see Jonathan Haidt, J. Patrick Seder, and Selin Kesebir, "Hive Psychology, Happiness, and Public Policy," *Journal of Legal Studies* (in press).

has a source outside myself. They would be good, or interesting, or worthwhile whether I liked or cared about or even noticed them or not. But they are values I *respond* to, for which I have an *affinity*. . . . (emphasis added)

But what would happen if we thought that the fundamental unit of society was not the individual but the group? What would happen if we looked at the long history of humanity on this planet and recognized our modern, independent sense of self as an historical and geographical anomaly? Cultural psychologists tell us that the independent, thick-walled self is the norm in Europe and in North America, but not elsewhere.[5] Historians tell us that Europeans developed this new, more differentiated, more independent self in the seventeenth and eighteenth centuries—a self that was more self-conscious, more prone to depression, and more likely to worry about finding the meaning of life.[6]

Why is it often painful to live in our modern, independent selves? I think the answer can be found in our origins. Many animals are social, but only a few are ultrasocial,[7] by which I mean that they live in groups of thousands, with extensive division of labor and a willingness to sacrifice and even die for the group. The best-known ultrasocial animals are bees, ants, termites, and naked mole rats. All of these creatures accomplish the trick of ultrasociality by being siblings who can only reproduce through a queen, or a single royal couple. It's one for all, all for one, and in a very real sense the hive is

---

[5] Hazel R. Markus and Shinobu Kitayama, "Culture and the Self: Implications for Cognition, Emotion, and Motivation," *Psychological Review* 98 (1991) 224–53.

[6] See review in Barbara Ehrenreich, *Dancing in the Streets: A History of Collective Joy* (New York: Metropolitan Books, 2006).

[7] Peter J. Richardson and Robert Boyd, "The Evolution of Human Ultra-Sociality," in *Indoctrinability, Ideology, and Warfare: Evolutionary Perspectives*, eds. I. Eibl-Eibesfeldt and F. K. Salter (New York: Berghahn, 1998) 71–95.

a superorganism. Bees are best understood as cells or organs within a larger body. The queen is not the brain of the hive, she is only its ovary.

Chimpanzees, by contrast, are social but not ultrasocial. They live in groups of a few dozen at most. They do not sacrifice their lives for others. They rarely even share food. Somehow our ancestors went from the moderate sociability of chimps to the ultrasociality we enjoy today. We humans live in groups much larger than can be explained through kinship; we divide labor, form teams and tribes, rally round the flag when attacked, do the wave at football games, dance the Macarena at weddings, and in a hundred other ways show that we were shaped by evolution to be selective ultra-socialists. We want, need, and love groups. We have special emotions that we feel only in groups. And we have special practices that bind groups together into a kind of hive. Barbara Ehrenreich recently made this case in her book *Dancing in the Streets: A History of Collective Joy*. She describes how collective, ecstatic dance used to be nearly a cultural universal, which functioned to soften hierarchy and bind groups together with love. But Europeans have long been ambivalent toward Dionysian tendencies, and Western psychology has ignored this side of our nature entirely. Ehrenreich writes that "if homosexual attraction is the love that 'dares not speak its name,' the love that binds people to the collective has no name at all to speak."[8]

Ehrenreich builds on an older book by the historian William McNeill, who first encountered the joy of synchronous movement during basic training for the army. After weeks of seemingly pointless drilling, his squadron finally got the synchrony right, and McNeill had a kind of mystical experience:

[8] Ehrenreich 14.

Words are inadequate to describe the emotion aroused by the prolonged movement in unison that drilling involved. A sense of pervasive well-being is what I recall; more specifically, a strange sense of personal enlargement; a sort of swelling out, becoming bigger than life, thanks to participation in collective ritual.[9]

McNeill argues that societies have always used synchronized motor movements, in dance, marching, bowing, and chanting, to create a social superorganism in which one loses oneself and finds joy and strength in becoming a cell in a larger body.

I raise these issues of ultrasociality and hive psychology because Wolf considers the popular advice to find meaning by getting involved with "something larger than oneself." She asks what size has to do with anything, and she concludes that the crucial thing is to get involved with something *outside* yourself.

I disagree. From the perspective of hive psychology, size matters a great deal. From the perspective of hive psychology, modern humans are essentially bees who busted out of the hive during the Enlightenment, and who burned down the last honeycombs during the twentieth century. We now fly around free and unencumbered, calling ourselves atheists, reading *Waiting for Godot*, and wondering, what does it all mean? Where can I find meaning? A good hive must be larger than one's self.

Conclusion

One of the great challenges of modernity is that we must now find hives for ourselves. We can't create them on our

---

[9] W. H. McNeill, *Keeping Together in Time: Dance and Drill in Human History* (Cambridge, MA: Harvard University Press, 1995) 2.

own any more than we can create a language on our own. But the view from positive psychology is that we can find meaning in life if we take advantage of our capacity for vital engagement and bind ourselves to projects and people. We can co-create, or join into, something larger than ourselves. We can join others in pursuit of common goals, nested in shared traditions and common values. Susan Wolf has done us a great service in showing us the challenges we face in choosing the right kind of hive, and in showing us why it matters that we choose rightly.

Response
Susan Wolf

I COULD NOT HAVE ASKED FOR a more gratifying set of commentaries. They are generous and constructive, challenging and provocative. Notably, every one of them stresses the importance of thinking about the question of meaning in life in a way that applies to real people, as opposed to people who are merely conceptually possible. (Indeed, they often refer to specific people, ranging from Henri Rousseau to Claus von Stauffenberg to a University of Virginia student.) Notably, too, they are graceful, witty, utterly free of jargon, and at the same time intellectually serious. Academic philosophy is often portrayed as pedantic, irrelevant, and incomprehensible to anyone outside the field. These commentaries prove that such charges are far from universally applicable. May they be an example and an inspiration both for those within and without the profession.

Gratifying, too, is the fact that my commentators divide in their assessments of my view of meaningfulness. John Koethe and Robert Adams, at least as I understand them, are fundamentally sympathetic to the central features of my view. They agree that meaning is fruitfully conceived in terms of appropriately interlocking subjective and objective elements. Their comments bring out issues within that basic framework that call for clarification, refinement, and decision. Nomy Arpaly and Jonathain Haidt are more skeptical of my principal thesis. Specifically, both question the need to refer to objective value in order to account for the distinction between a meaningful and a meaningless life that I am concerned to understand. Writing independently but in ways that are importantly related, they offer alternative explanations of the phenomena I discuss that are compatible with a purely subjective account of meaningfulness. Though someone unfamiliar with philosophical practice might have expected that one would want one's listeners, readers, and commentators universally to agree with one's primary theses, from my perspective the range of responses in these commentaries is far preferable. That two distinguished philosophers find the basic idea of these lectures plausible and fruitful allows me to put to rest doubts that my views are wildly absurd, so obviously wrong as to be not worth pursuing. At the same time, the fact that two other first-rate minds are inclined to contest these views reassures me that my thoughts on meaningfulness are not so obvious as to be not worth mentioning, or so uncontroversial as to make the idea of arguing for them otiose.

Let me begin by responding to Koethe and Adams, whose commentaries accept the general framework of my view, raising questions internal to it. With me, they grant that a meaningful life must satisfy both objective and subjective conditions, suitably linked, but they press me (and others) to consider more closely just how much and what kind of objective value and subjective experience is necessary. I welcome the chance to elaborate and reconsider my views on these matters, but I should add that it is in the spirit of my enterprise to invite a conversation on these issues. Within the general framework of the idea of meaningfulness I have argued for, my own opinions on the finer points are not privileged.

A Question about the Objective Component of Meaningfulness: How Important Is Success?

One of the most important topics requiring elaboration is the question of the relevance (to meaningfulness) of the success of one's projects and goals. As John Koethe points out, the claim that meaningfulness is a matter of active engagement in "projects of objective value" is ambiguous. Making art and raising a family may be said to be objectively valuable projects by contrast to cultivating one's prowess at long-distance spitting or collecting a big ball of string. To say this is to say that they are valuable *kinds* of projects; the other kinds, not so much. But a project that is of a valuable kind may yet be successful or unsuccessful. One may create a masterpiece, a modestly good work, or mere drivel or noise. One may nurture a family with love and support, bringing out the best in one's children and partner and helping them to flourish, or one may, despite the best of intentions, make a mess of things, contributing to one's family's dysfunction, inhibiting one's children's development, creating an atmosphere of insecurity and distrust. Even if my lectures emphasized the importance to meaningfulness of being engaged in valuable *kinds* of projects and activities, Koethe is right to surmise that I take the success of these projects and activities to be relevant as well. Since meaningfulness on my view is meant to answer concerns about whether one's life can be seen as a proper source of pride, one that can be judged to be good from a detached perspective, this is what one would expect. But what kind and degree of success is necessary for a life to be satisfactorily meaningful? This is a difficult question.

Our most obvious paradigms of meaningful lives are the lives of people whose (valuable kinds of) projects are successful: artists who create good art; scientists and scholars who advance our knowledge and understanding; politicians and activists who reduce injustice; physicians who heal; teachers who educate; lovers and friends, parents and children who appreciate and enhance the lives of those they love. Consider, however, the lives of people who do not succeed. Are they less meaningful? Why or why not?

Think first about how the person herself would feel upon learning that a project in which she has been deeply invested has failed: the scientist whose life's work has come to naught, or been superseded by another colleague's results; the farmer whose farm, which he had hoped to hand down to his children, goes into foreclosure; the woman who, after years of sacrifice and devotion, discovers that the man around whom she has built her life has been lying to her and using her all along. If these people were to think of their lives as wasted, a total loss, it would not be unnatural or surprising, and such a thought is at least somewhat akin to the thought that one's life (or this period of it) has been meaningless. To deny that the success or failure of such projects is relevant to the meaningfulness of one's life would fly in the face of such reasonable reactions. Yet most people would resist the judgment that these agents might be inclined to make of their own lives in the immediate aftermath of their projects' failures. It is instructive to reflect on the sorts of things we might say to convince them (or ourselves) that their verdict is too harsh.

Thus, for example, in the case of the scientist, we might point out that though she did not obtain the specific results she had hoped for, she did play a part in the overall scientific enterprise. The advance of science (and, for that matter, of art) depends on an ongoing community of people, practices, institutions, working in interlocking ways on a variety of projects. Her project may have failed according to the description she would likely have applied to what she was doing—"trying to discover protein X," say, or "trying to find a new way to measure Y"—but there are other descriptions, which she would also have recognized as valid, such as "doing scientific research," which point to ways in which her activities remain at least somewhat valuable. Further, we might remind her that in the course of pursuing her overall goal, she had to engage in a variety of subsidiary activities, subprojects with smaller or overlapping aims, including many that involved other people, such as technicians, postdoctoral researchers, and graduate students. Such relationships and encounters can be positive or negative. They may educate, advance, or improve the quality of life of those with whom the scientist interacts, or they may impede, defeat, or mislead them. If the scientist has helped or encouraged those around her, she has presumably done so intentionally, even if not very self-consciously, and there is value and meaning in that. Finally, it is at least arguable that the exercise of virtue and talent—of intellectual creativity and integrity, of patience, discipline, and determination—has value in itself.

When the scientist looks back at this portion of her life, she may continue to feel disappointed. How much better she would feel about herself and about her years of work and sacrifice if they had yielded a useful result for which she could have taken credit! Still, the idea that those years were wasted, that the period devoted to her unsuccessful efforts was meaningless, seems inordinately negative. If in addition, the research project that itself was a failure points the way to future research or puts her life on a path from which new projects of value emerge, the retrospective assessment of this period of her life will be so much the more positive. Learning from mistakes, failures, and disappointments allows us to redeem periods of our lives that would appear as total losses if viewed in isolation.

The sorts of considerations we have raised in reflecting on the scientist's failed projects give an indication of how we might assess the other examples of failure mentioned above. Ultimately, only the details of a particular case can determine what kind and degree of meaning can be salvaged from a project that, under its primary description, must be deemed a failure. Often, if the project is of a good kind—if, in other words, the subject is engaged in activities that if successful would be nonegocentrically valuable—then *something* of value is achieved in the very commitment to that project and in the striving to pursue it, which will be a sufficiently intentional part of the agent's activities and values to contribute a measure of meaningfulness to that period of the person's life.

In the case of Claus von Stauffenberg, such considerations are exceptionally convincing, providing us with plenty of reasons to support Robert Adams's claim that in Stauffenberg we see that "a life can derive meaning of the greatest value from a project that failed." Though the plot to assassinate Hitler did fail—and even, as Adams reminds us, led to hundreds of deaths—the eventual publicity that the plot garnered did show the world that not all Germans were either Nazis or cowards, thus achieving at least one of the goals that Stauffenberg thought important. Moreover, even if the plot had been suppressed, and the world had never learned of the attempt, the vision, the integrity, and the courage that Stauffenberg displayed were extraordinary and heroic, giving him the resources to look back on his life with a degree not of consolation only but of pride that most of us are not in a position to claim even if our less demanding projects are successful.

It is harder to know what to say about the situation of artists with the kind of ambition to which Koethe directs our attention. Koethe may be right that it is inherent in projects such as these that one cannot know whether they are successful, or even be clear about what would constitute success. Moreover, unlike Stauffenberg, whose project was such that we could be confident in advance that even if it failed, it would at least be a noble failure, an artist with great ambition may be merely deluded. This implies, as Koethe realizes, that one whose life is built around such a project might not be able to know, and so a fortiori not be able to get joy or satisfaction from the knowledge that his life is meaningful (even if it is). With Koethe, I think this is a possibility that we simply have to live with. Those who are driven to such a life, who aspire to this sort of achievement, are not likely to be deterred by the consideration that they must live with that kind of uncertainty in their self-assessment.

There are many more facets to the question of what kinds and degree of objective value contribute to the meaningfulness of a life that we might explore. Many of them are interesting and provocative, and there may be good reasons to pursue them. But it is useful to bear in mind that the point of articulating a conception of meaningfulness is not to enable us to rank actual or possible lives along some scale of meaningfulness. It is easy to get sucked into the activity of rating lives, comparing them, and debating borderline cases. Is the life of a minor poet (in the good sense, that Koethe recognizes as a significant achievement) any less meaningful than that of a major one? How does the life of a housecleaner or an aerobics instructor or a truck driver compare to the life of a Supreme Court Justice or a freedom fighter? Does the meaningfulness of one's own life depend on how one's children turn out? There may be no answer to some of these questions, and no point to pursuing them, even if there are answers.

In offering an account of meaning, I have been mainly concerned to bring out and illuminate the existence of this dimension of value in a life, distinct as it is from both happiness and morality. I have argued that there is more to life than pleasure and duty, and have sketched an account of another dimension along which a life may be better or worse. These thoughts may come in handy in reflecting on and directing one's life, in guiding the lives of one's children and students, in shaping social institutions, and in formulating political goals. Moreover, as I argued in the second lecture, without the concept of meaningfulness and a vocabulary with which to discuss and explore it, we are apt to accept distorted conceptions of happiness and morality, to seek the wrong things, and to be at a loss to understand what is going wrong. None of this, however, requires that we undertake detailed assessments of other people's lives. Nor should it be assumed that, with respect to our own lives and the lives of those we love, there is any strong reason to try to maximize meaningfulness. Though it seems to me a great good that one's life be meaningful, and not just barely, minimally meaningful, but robustly meaningful, it may nonetheless not be reasonable or even intelligible to care that one's life be as meaningful as possible.

A Question about the Subjective Component of Meaningfulness: How Important Is Fulfillment?

Along with questions about what kinds of objective achievements are necessary for a meaningful life, Adams's comments press me to revise and clarify my description of the subjective condition that, according to my view, a meaningful life must meet. In my lectures, I frequently identified the subjective condition with the experience of fulfillment, but, as Adams brings out, that term is misleading, and my discussion of the subjective condition is in many ways crude. Referring to fulfillment as "a good feeling," for example, underemphasizes the intentionality of the condition (the fact that one must be fulfilled *by* something, that one must find some experience or activity fulfilling), and may encourage too close an association between what I mean by fulfillment and feelings of pleasure. At the same time, the term "fulfillment" has an unwanted association with the idea of success. To fulfill a dream or a responsibility, after all, is successfully to realize or complete or discharge it. If one agrees with Adams—and who would not?—that Stauffenberg might correctly have regarded his life as meaningful, even at its end, then one must admit that a life can both be and seem meaningful in virtue of engagement in projects which the subject would be unlikely to describe either as fulfilling or as making him feel good. Indeed, Adams goes so far as to suggest that it might be better to drop the condition of fulfillment altogether. Why is it not enough to emphasize that meaningful projects are those to which the agent is attached through reasons and motives of love? Since love also has a subjective component, such a revision would retain the important idea that meaningfulness is a matter of being subjectively connected with objectively valuable activity in the right way, but it would remove the suggestion that a meaningful life is especially likely to be a contented one.

To a large extent, I agree with Adams's suggestions. Wanting to recognize the subjective dimension of meaningfulness, I settled on the term "fulfillment" as a way to designate the qualitative character essential to a meaningful life, and I described it as "a good feeling" both to emphasize that it *is* a subjective or qualitative feature that I am talking about and to bring out how peculiar it would be to value the subjective feature on its own, pared away from any assumptions about the objective nature of the activities or relationships by which one was fulfilled. But to so describe the range of ways in which a person might experience a meaningful life is unrealistic and simplistic, and Adams is right to point out the inadequacy of my characterization. Though it is central to my view that there is a subjective dimension to meaningfulness, there is no reason to believe or expect that there is a single subjective quality of experience that all meaningful lives possess (even if one had a clearer grasp than I do of the identity conditions of a quality of experience in the first place).

In my lectures, I used a variety of terms to refer to the subjective dimension of meaningfulness: in addition to fulfillment, I spoke of subjective attraction, of being gripped or excited by one's projects and activities, and of loving them. Though there are connections and overlaps between these psychological conditions, they are hardly synonymous. Moreover, many if not most projects and activities that contribute to the meaningfulness of one's life will not be gripping, exciting, or subjectively fulfilling at every instant of engagement. In the course of writing a book, training for a marathon, not to mention raising a child, there may be moments or even long periods of frustration or ambivalence. Proofreading and indexing can be boring; sitting in rush hour traffic to pick one's child up from her music lessons can be maddening. During a slump, a person may feel alienated from all her projects, only to recover her sense of meaningfulness later without making any change at all in the nature of the projects.

Still, if one *usually* finds her daily activities boring, if she typically feels alienated from the roles and projects that she is nonetheless bound to occupy and pursue, if she is inclined to describe herself as feeling empty or even dead inside as she goes through the motions of her life, then that life is less than satisfactorily meaningful, even if what she is doing is

objectively valuable and she recognizes that this is so. The
various attitudes I mentioned in my discussion of the subjective aspect of meaningfulness reflect the idea that the
subjective character of meaningful activity (that is, of the
experience of engagement in activities that contribute to
meaningfulness in one's life) are, for the most part, at the
opposite end of the spectrum from attitudes like boredom,
emptiness, and alienation.

It is notable that these attitudes and qualities—of excitement, of being gripped by or "into" a project, of experiencing
flow, of loving what one is doing, of finding an activity or
pursuit fulfilling—are not in themselves forms of pleasure
in the standard sense of that term. Excitement is compatible
with fear; love is compatible with sadness; the activities one
finds fulfilling are perhaps more often than not difficult and
demanding. Still, just as boredom, emptiness, and alienation,
though not precisely painful, are extremely undesirable ways
to feel over large segments of one's life, attitudes of love, fulfillment, and active engagement are positive, desirable, good
aspects of experience. They are, in that sense "good feelings,"
desirable in themselves, at least when they are directed toward and generated by appropriate objects and activities.[1]

Adams suggests that rather than adopt "fulfillment" as the
(now admittedly imperfect) catch-all term for the subjective
side of meaningful activity, I might have stopped with my
opening claim that meaning comes from acting on reasons of
love. Perhaps he is right. Love, like fulfillment, is quite obviously intentional and, when felt toward an appropriate object,
positive. Furthermore, since it is well known that there are

[1] Another ready stock of examples that support the idea that qualitative experiences that are not straightforwardly pleasurable may nonetheless be noninstrumen-
tally desirable can be found in aesthetics; for example, in the experience of beautiful
sad music, of powerful tragic drama, of terrifying horror films.

various ways one might feel about people and activities one loves,[2] "love" is perhaps less likely than "fulfillment" to be misunderstood to indicate a single specific qualitative feeling that must accompany or complete all cases of meaningful activity, much less to be confused with easy pleasure.

However, there are some lives whose principal activities and projects are shaped and guided by love in a sense, which nonetheless are far from paradigmatically meaningful. The alienated housewife might genuinely love her husband and children; the conscripted soldier might truly love his country. Perhaps because of their love, they regard it as their duty to respond respectively to their family's or their country's need. Nonetheless, the woman is not cut out to be a homemaker, or the boy to fight in a war. They may feel trapped by their circumstances, compelled to live in ways that leave them no opportunity to pursue their passions or to realize their potentials. They might well describe their lives as lacking in meaning (even though it would be going too far to describe them as utterly meaningless); but it would be simply wrong to describe them as lacking in love.

When considering cases like these, focusing on feelings of fulfillment seems apt. It is the absence of such feelings (as opposed to the absence of love, for example) that indicates that there is an important good missing in these lives that is not captured by our ordinary understanding of happiness, but which cannot be cashed out purely in terms of objective value either.[3] More generally, when a person is dissatisfied

[2] See for example, David Velleman, "Love as a Moral Emotion," *Ethics* 109 (January 1999).

[3] It is not clear whether Adams would agree with me. His remark, in an earlier draft of his comment, that "an action done from love with grim determination . . . can contribute to the meaningfulness of a life," suggests that he might characterize the alienated soldier and homemaker as living meaningful lives despite their feelings of dissatisfaction.

with her own life in a way that she might describe in terms of a yearning for meaning, I suspect it is fulfillment rather than love that she experiences herself as lacking. Conceptually, fulfillment is much more closely connected to meaning than love. Indeed, it seems to be hard to separate the idea that one finds an activity or relationship fulfilling from the thought that the person regards the activity as meaningful.

Still, as Adams has shown, there are other cases in which the description of a person's engagement in meaningful activities as fulfilling seems forced. Rather than continue the search for a single term to name an attitude or psychological condition that any meaningful life must involve, it might be wiser, if less satisfyingly determinate, simply to acknowledge that there is a range of such attitudes and conditions, which includes love and fulfillment, and which reflects the kind of intentional, but also qualitatively positive, attachment to an object or activity that an agent must have in order for engagement with it to contribute to the meaningfulness of his life.[4]

In the course of his discussion of the subjective component of meaningfulness, Adams raises one more question that I would like to address before moving on to other topics—namely, the question of *when* in a person's life his attitude toward his activities and projects is relevant. While engaged in an (objectively valuable) project or activity, a person may find it fulfilling, even though he later comes to dismiss it as

---

[4] It would be helpful, of course, to be able to say something more about what kind of attachment is necessary. In her recent dissertation, "An Account of Valuing" (University of North Carolina, 2008), Anabella Zagura argues that valuing is essential to a person's ability to live a meaningful life, understanding valuing to be neither a matter of belief nor of desire, but of a kind of commitment to seeing the object of value as valuable. This seems to me a promising approach for getting to the bottom of the subjective attachment that is common to love and fulfillment.

meaningless;[5] conversely, he may regard a task as drudgery for many years, only to recognize its worth later in life and to take pride in having completed it. With Adams, I agree that one may (correctly) "find one's life meaningful *in* living it, regardless of how it will seem in one's retrospective view." Presumably, the kind of meaning one finds *in* living is the most desirable kind to have. Nonetheless, I do not want to refuse all credibility to a person's retrospective evaluation. If a person looking back correctly finds value in having done something with a part of her life that she did not regard as meaningful at the time, this seems to me to count for something in the overall assessment of her life's meaningfulness. It is not obvious how best to weigh the various perspectives a person may have on the meaningfulness of her own life, or on periods of it, in forming such an assessment. Similar puzzles arise with respect to the differing perspectives people tend to have on their own happiness,[6] which I also find deeply puzzling. We should, however, also be mindful that such overall assessments of the meaningfulness of people's lives are of limited interest.

Reasons of Meaning and Reasons of Love

Indeed, as Nomy Arpaly points out, people who live meaningful lives may not think or care very much about the meaning of their lives. One gets meaning from acting on reasons of love, but the love at issue is love of the activity or the

---

[5] Tolstoy seems to have had an experience of this nature: Leo Tolstoy, *My Confession* (London: J. M. Dent and Sons, 1905). Reprinted in ed. E. D. Klemke, *The Meaning of Life* (New York: Oxford University Press, 1981) 9–19.

[6] See, *e.g.*, Daniel Kahneman and Jason Riis, "Living, and Thinking About It: Two Perspectives on Life," in eds. F. Huppert, N. Baylis, and B. Kaverne, *The Science of Wellbeing: Integrating Neurobiology, Psychology and Social Science* (Oxford: Oxford University Press, 2005) and David Velleman, "Well-Being and Time," *Pacific Philosophical Quarterly* 72 (1991).

person or ideal or goal that defines or structures the activity. It is not love of meaning itself or of the value of living a meaningful life. As Arpaly says, "Those who act for the love of art do not act for the sake of a meaningful life but rather for the sake of art." When one helps a friend, it is love of the friend that moves one to act and not love of the meaning that the friendship brings to one's life.

In my lectures I was regrettably unclear about the relation between reasons of love and what might be called reasons of meaning, and about the corresponding relation between the value of the objects of love and the value of a meaningful life. Arpaly's comments are a useful corrective, and point to the need to say more.

At the beginning of my lectures, I argued that many of the reasons and motives on which we act are neither reasons of self-interest nor reasons of morality. Rather, I suggested, they are grounded in personal attachments to objects, activities, and ideals. I called them "reasons of love." By noting that acting on behalf of such reasons, when the objects, activities, and so on are worthy, brings meaning to our lives, I meant not only to call attention to this range of reasons and motives, but also to bring out their significance and to defend their legitimacy. I have also been arguing throughout these lectures that meaning is an important dimension of a good life, distinct from the other important dimensions of self-interest and morality. But I did not mean to suggest that reasons (and motives) of love were good reasons only or even primarily *because* having them and acting on them contributes to (and indeed is essential to) meaning in our lives. The relation between meaning and reasons of love is quite different from the relation between self-interest and, say, reasons of pleasure, and between morality and, say, reasons of kindness. Let me explain.

When one gets a pizza or goes for a walk or takes a vacation because one expects it to be pleasurable, one acts on what might be called reasons of pleasure. One is motivated by the thought that the action will be fun or relaxing, or that it will relieve the pain of hunger. One may never class these acts under the more general and abstract heading of "self-interest." But generally, one would be willing to acknowledge one's reasons of pleasure as a species of reasons of self-interest. If one came to be convinced that the anticipated pleasures were not going to be conducive to one's overall well-being, one would typically take this to be a strong reason to reconsider one's decision. Similarly, when one comforts a child who has skinned his knee, shovels the driveway of an elderly neighbor, or gives money to a homeless person collecting coins on the street, one acts on what might be called reasons of kindness. One may never class these acts under the more general and abstract heading of "morality." But generally, one would be willing to acknowledge one's reasons of kindness as a species of moral reasons. If one came to be convinced that the actions one was contemplating would not be recommended or even permitted by morality overall, one would typically take this to be a strong reason to reconsider one's decision. As Arpaly points out, the relation between meaning and reasons of love (the sorts of reasons that in fact are necessary to give meaning to one's life) is less direct. Reasons of love are not a *species* of reasons of meaning: when one visits one's brother, or helps one's friend, or labors over one's philosophy article, one does not ordinarily do it in order to give meaning to one's life or as an expression of one's interest in living a meaningful life. If one were to conclude (rightly or wrongly) that the contemplated action was not likely to make one's life more meaningful, that conclusion would not necessarily speak strongly against the action. It would seem rather beside the point.

Insofar as there are such things as "reasons of meaning"—that is, insofar as facts to the effect that something will contribute to the meaning of a person's life give reasons to foster or promote that thing, those facts will rarely be directly available to the people whose lives are in question and are not likely to matter much, even when they are. At least if my conception of meaningfulness is right, those acts which contribute to meaningfulness in a person's life will be connected to loves or passions for things that the person recognizes as independently valuable. She will therefore have other reasons, not connected to her life's meaning, to do them, and the question of their relation to her life's meaning will not arise.

The importance of meaning as a dimension of a good life, and of the weight and legitimacy of reasons to promote it is apt to be of more practical relevance in other contexts. When advising or judging others, I have argued, the fact that something they want to do will contribute to their lives' meaning gives us different and in some cases stronger reasons to encourage or permit it than we would have if their actions would make them happy in other ways. (Thus, we are more tolerant of someone's missing office hours to attend a lecture than to soak in a hot bath; more tolerant of someone lying to protect a friend than lying to protect herself.) Further, considerations of meaning may be relevant to making decisions that bear, at a more abstract level, on the question of how to shape one's life or raise one's children, as well as to questions of larger scope about how to structure educational institutions and shape social policy. Recognizing that meaningfulness is a dimension of a good life distinct from happiness, and that meaning arises when subjective attraction meets objective attractiveness will give parents a reason to expose their children to a range of worthwhile activities and projects to which they might be "subjectively attracted" (that is, about which they might get passionate). Indeed, it will make one want to ensure that all children are exposed to such things, and that our social, political, and economic institutions provide opportunities for all people to form relations and pursue interests that bring meaning to their lives as well as pleasure and comfort. To a considerable extent, we already want these things. This is at least part of why we give our children music lessons, support arts programs in the schools, and approve of spending to maintain national parks. To that extent, my identification and analysis of the dimension of meaning may simply make explicit what lies behind these concerns and what is at stake if we fail to address them.

A Challenge to the Fitting Fulfillment View: Is Objective Value Really Necessary for Meaning?

But is my view of meaningfulness in life correct? Does a meaningful life really require active and loving engagement in projects of worth? More specifically, do we really need to commit ourselves to the objectivity of values inherent in the notion of "projects of worth" in order to distinguish meaningful from meaningless lives? Jonathan Haidt's and Nomy Arpaly's commentaries both raise this challenge, in remarkably similar and mutually reinforcing ways.

Both Haidt and Arpaly begin their critiques by accepting the intuitive judgments of individual lives that I offered along the way to developing my view of meaning. That is, they agree that, other things being equal, a life spent caring for a pet goldfish or entering lawn mower races is not likely to be as meaningful as one spent writing symphonies or directing a youth group. Both suggest, however, that we can account for these judgments on a purely empirical basis. As Arpaly points out, "much of Goldfish Nut's brain remains unused. She does not experience the satisfaction of learning or even of gradually becoming better at a task . . . . Basic emotional needs, even very general and disjunctive ones, remain unsatisfied for her." And Haidt notes that "lawn mower racing and flagpole-sitting do not lend themselves to vital engagement." Their point, I take it, is that normal human beings are simply not fulfilled by these activities. They are neither complex enough nor social enough to be satisfying, at least as activities around which to build an entire life. No reference to objective value is needed to make or to establish these claims. We can simply observe human behavior. Thus, the simple Fulfillment View can validate these intuitive judgments without needing to go out on a metaethical limb.

Haidt's and Arpaly's discussions of human psychology are insightful and instructive, with interesting implications, I believe, for the Fitting Fulfillment View. Still, I believe there are reasons to resist using their insights to defend a fulfillment view of meaning that is independent of any reference to objective value.

At first glance, Arpaly's and Haidt's discussions may suggest a view of meaningfulness that seems gratuitously to privilege the normal. Arpaly writes explicitly: "about the *normal* adult human who receives full satisfaction in her life from keeping a goldfish: she does not exist." And Haidt asks of the lawn mower racers and flagpole-sitters, "How may of them found flow in these activities as adolescents, devoured all the books they could find on the history of lawn mowers and flagpoles, lovingly assembled collections of lawn mowers and flagpoles, and chose colleges and jobs so as to ensure that they would always be able to race mowers or sit on poles in the company of other mower-racers and pole-sitters?" The answer, presumably, is "very few." But, a reader might reasonably ask, what of it? What is so good about being normal? In the absence of an answer, one needs some further explanation of why these activities do not provide meaning for those who *do* find them fulfilling—or, alternatively, of the conditions under which they do.

Looking more closely at Haidt's and Arpaly's commentaries, one sees that their remarks offer the beginnings of an answer to these demands. Both refer to standard human needs and capacities that will not ordinarily be met or exercised by engagement in the quirky projects that we intuitively feel are not fit sources of meaning. They implicitly suggest that it is the fulfillment of these needs and the exercise of these capacities that is the real key to meaningfulness. If, contrary to statistics, caring for a goldfish (as in Arpaly's example of the retarded child) or racing lawn mowers does form the core of a pattern of activities that meets these needs satisfactorily, then the project which might have seemed silly in abstraction, will after all give meaning to the subject's life.

Their discussions usefully bring out the resources that a defender of a (simple) Fulfillment View has for responding to the thought experiments I posed in my lectures. Indeed, as I have interpreted their commentaries, they suggest a version of the simple Fulfillment View that is both different from and richer than the view that I presented in my lectures, and well worth elaborating as an alternative view deserving serious consideration. By connecting fulfillment with the meeting of psychological needs (for example, for companionship) and the exercise of human capacities (of vital engagement, perhaps), or, more generally, with the realization of a natural human potential, this view may be understood to interpret fulfillment not as a purely subjective feature, a matter of the qualitative character of the subject's experience, but rather as a more substantial, objective condition. Thus, for example, according to this view, if humans have a need for love and intimacy, then a fulfilling life must include love and intimacy—*feeling* that one has love and intimacy, if one is deceived, would not satisfy this condition.

If I understand Haidt and Arpaly correctly, they are suggesting that we understand fulfillment in this way, and that we identify the meaningfulness of a person's life with her being fulfilled according to this conception. Though fulfillment, according to this view, is an objective condition, involving perhaps the requirements that a subject *be* loved, intellectually challenged, vitally engaged, rather than just believing or feeling herself to be so, it requires no reference or commitment to objective *values*. This view, which understands fulfillment roughly as realization of a being's psychological nature, is part of a venerable tradition that can be traced at least as far back as Aristotle.[7] As a conception of what it is for a being to be fulfilled, there is much to be said on its behalf. There are, however, several reasons for resisting identifying fulfillment, so understood, with meaning in life.

First, although this view does not privilege the normal, it does privilege the natural, for it identifies fulfillment with meeting the demands of one's (human) nature. Leaving aside the difficulty of determining what constitutes human nature, the question remains, What is so good about doing what it is in one's nature to do? Does it matter what kind of nature one has? Does it matter, for example, whether one's nature is peaceable or belligerent, creative or imitative, social or solitary? These questions are especially pressing if we identify fulfillment with meaningfulness. Even if one can defend the idea that realizing the potentials of one's nature is a form of fulfillment that contributes to the good of the

---

[7] It finds more recent expression in Joel Feinberg's wonderful essay, "Absurd Self-Fulfillment," in Feinberg, *Freedom & Fulfillment* (Princeton: Princeton University Press, 1982).

subject, and thus is an ingredient of her self-interest, it is
not obvious why it would make the person's life meaningful.
Moreover, if it is possible to transcend one's nature, and to
do something wonderful that is not connected to one's nature, shouldn't that too be a way in which that person's life
can be made meaningful?

These questions reflect the possibility of looking at and assessing a person (oneself or another) from a perspective that
is not confined to self-interest.[8] We can ask not only whether
a person's life, or a given portion of it, has been good for him
or her, but whether it has been admirable, a life (or portion of
a life) that the person can be proud of. In my lectures, I suggested that the desire to be able to see one's own life as good
from this perspective is common and deep, and I pointed out
that living a meaningful life, as I understand meaningfulness,
responds to that desire. A second reason for not wanting to
identify meaningfulness with fulfillment of the demands and
potentials of one's nature (whatever they are) is that it would
sever this connection, leaving this perspective unnamed and
potentially forgotten.

Haidt suspects that I fear that "if there is no such thing as
objective value, then . . . lawn mower racing, flagpole-sitting,
and rock rolling will have just as strong a claim to being
meaningful as writing a symphony or righting an injustice."
I confess to a prereflective suspicion that lawn mower racing
is less likely to give meaning to a life than musical compo-
sition; my interest, however, is in *understanding* my initial
suspicion, not in confirming it. For the reasons I offered in
my lectures, I arrived at a conception that I found plausible:
that meaning comes from active engagement in projects of

---

[8] This is not to say that an assessment from this perspective is irrelevant to the
person's self-interest, however.

objective worth. If it should turn out that lawn mover racing *has* (or has a place in a web of activities that have) objective worth, rather than being merely a whimsical and harmless kind of fun, then, on my conception, it *will* contribute meaning to the lives of those who appreciate and respond to that value. There is nothing to fear in that.

Haidt meanwhile expresses his own fear of what he takes to be a consequence of my view. Specifically, he fears that "if someone ever does come up with an adequate theory of objective value," [I might have to tell his] former student "that her love of horses is in danger of being declared meaningless." I believe this fear is unfounded for several reasons.

First, no one need accept someone else's word for what has objective value. No one has the authority to "declare" to another person what has and what lacks objective value. In articulating his fear, Haidt conjures up the image of a philosopher, or perhaps a jury of philosophers, who claim expertise not only in how to make sense of the *idea* of objective value, but also in how to apply it. He is rightly resistant to this idea. As I said in my lectures, I believe that the question of what projects and activities are objectively worthwhile is open to anyone and everyone to ask and try to answer, and we are likely to make the most progress toward an answer if we pool our information and experience. The history of culture and of morals makes amply clear that if there is such a thing as objective worth, we are very fallible guides to determining which activities and objects have it. It is only sensible that if we are interested in determining whether a particular activity or set of activities is worthwhile, we should seek the perspectives of those who are most familiar with it. If Haidt's student *finds* something valuable in her web of horse-riding projects, she may be able to articulate it and make the value intelligible even to those who are initially skeptical. Moreover, even should she be unable to convince others, this does not imply that she must be mistaken.

At the same time, my insistence on linking the question of meaning with the question of objective worth implies that the question of whether one's life is meaningful is essentially risky. There is always some chance that what one thinks is valuable will turn out not to be, that the objects of one's subjective attraction will turn out not to be objectively attractive. One might be worshipping a false god, loving a scoundrel, writing terrible poetry.[9] In urging that we take note of meaningfulness as a distinctive dimension of a good life, to be identified with loving engagement in projects of worth, I am implicitly encouraging people to face that risk—that is, to ask whether their projects are projects of worth.

A second reason, therefore, that I do not share Haidt's fear for his student is that it does not seem to me a bad thing for her to ask the question whether it is worthwhile to spend her life engaged in the interlocking activities that center around a love of riding horses, no matter what answer she comes to. When analytic philosophers step back and ask whether they are doing anything valuable, whether their books, their courses, their projects are worthwhile, their concern strikes most people as appropriate if not positively commendable. If they are able to answer the question affirmatively, the self-conscious understanding of why what they are doing is worthwhile will add at least to the satisfaction they get from their philosophical activities if not to the quality of those activities themselves. Alternatively, reflection on this question may lead to mixed results, leading them to alter the topics on which they concentrate their research, or to adjust

---

[9] Indeed, the special riskiness of ambitious art projects is the central theme of John Koethe's commentary.

their writing style, or to shift the proportions of the time they devote to teaching, service, and research. If reflection on the worth of what one is doing is appropriate and potentially beneficial for analytic philosophers, I do not see why it would not be equally so for equestrians.

To be sure, there is the possibility, or risk, that reflection on one's cherished activities will lead one to conclude that the activities have little or no worth beyond the pleasure one gets from engaging in them. Even this conclusion, in my opinion, need not be cause for despair. Though I was concerned in my lectures to insist that meaningfulness is an important dimension of a good life, the distinctiveness of which has been frequently overlooked, I did not mean to suggest that it is the *only* good in life or that given the choice between doing something that would enhance the meaningfulness of one's life and doing something that would realize or support some other of one's values, the more meaningful alternative ought always to win out. (The questions with which Nomy Arpaly concludes her commentary suggest that my lectures were unclear on this point.) Getting pleasure from an activity is a perfectly good reason for engaging in it. If the activity is harmless and does not crowd out all significant opportunities for meaning, there is no reason not to spend time engaged in it "merely" for fun.

Furthermore, both my commentators and I have tended in our remarks to discuss people as if their lives were properly characterized as having one dominant project or interest, on which the meaningfulness of their lives was understood to stand or fall. We should recognize the artificiality of such characterizations, especially if we mean to apply these ideas to real or realistic characters and to assess the meaningfulness of their lives as wholes. We have written as if a person is either A Poet *or* A Parent, A Caretaker of Goldfish *or* A

Rider of Horses. By focusing on one activity or project at a time, or on lives that are predominantly bound up with a single project, we were able to illustrate and test our ideas more clearly and more vividly than if we had discussed lives that were, or were noticed to be, more complex and varied. But most lives *are* more complex and varied. We have multiple roles, relationships, projects, and interests. We have families, friends, coworkers, neighbors; we belong to book clubs, church groups, bowling leagues, and neighborhood associations; we listen to music, knit, garden, jog; we read the comics every morning, do the crossword puzzle every night.

Some of the activities and rituals that make up our lives may have solely instrumental value—they keep us healthy and sharpen skills that allow us to go on to do other things, and some may provide exclusively egocentric satisfactions. Many of the things we do, however, even those we do primarily for instrumental or hedonistic reasons, also have some independent value. In a typical multifaceted life, one's sources of meaning are not all in one proverbial basket. Assessing such a life for meaningfulness, one need not place too much stock in any one activity or project. A third reason not to fear for Jonathan Haidt's student, then, is that even if she doubts that her horse-related activities have any objective worth, this need not be a reason to give them up or to feel guilty about continuing them. In a multifaceted life, not *every* activity need contribute to meaning, much less contribute greatly to meaning, in order for a commitment to it to be justified.

The Interdependence of Objective Value and Subjective Interest—A Reconciliation?

In fact, however, I suspect that the relationships Haidt's student has to riding, to her horse, and to horses more generally, do have value, and that the web of activities she has built around these relationships contributes to the meaningfulness as well as the happiness or fulfillment of her life. (I suspect the same goes for the web of activities that analytic philosophers build around their enthusiasm for philosophy.) Indeed, as I mentioned in my lectures, I am inclined to think that almost anything to which a significant number of people have shown themselves to be deeply attached over a significant length of time, has or relates to some positive value—that almost anything people *find* valuable (stably and in significant numbers), *is* valuable. In my lectures, I expanded on this thought by focusing on the likelihood that the objects of such attachments had qualities that made them worthy of interest independently of whether anyone actually noticed those qualities. If people find an object or activity or project engaging, I suggested, there is apt to be something about it that makes it so. Perhaps the activity is challenging, or the object beautiful, or the project morally important. Haidt's discussion of vital engagement, however, as well as Arpaly's description of the retarded child whose life is enriched and, plausibly, made more meaningful through caring for a goldfish, suggest a different possible relationship between the objects of people's subjective attractions and their objective worth that is at least as important.

Both Haidt's and Arpaly's discussions remind us of the fact that when people get deeply interested in something and come to care about it, they focus their attention on it, build activities around it, exercise and sharpen their skills in advancing, protecting, and celebrating it. Further, they invite and encourage others to share their enthusiasm, creating new relationships and social groups, and forging or reinforcing bonds in existing relationships through shared activities and the shared appreciation of a common object. Even if the object upon which the attention is focused is initially of no particular value, those who come to be engaged with it may build a network of valuable activities around it, involving the development and exercise of skills (the realization of one's human potential), and the flowering and strengthening of positive human relationships.

Sports and games offer ready examples of the kind of relationship between objects of interest and their value that I have in mind. Presumably, there is nothing especially valuable about a group of people running around, trying to throw a ball into a hoop, while another group runs around trying to stop them. Nor does the adoption of extra rules, constraining the moves that are permitted, lift their running around into the category of practices that in themselves the participants have reason to be proud of from a detached perspective. Even if basketball, removed or abstracted from its now established place in our culture, is not an objectively valuable activity in itself, it provides an opportunity for much that is of value. It provides an opportunity for the cultivation and exercise of skill and virtue, for the building of relationships, and for the communion that comes from enthusiasm for and immersion in a shared activity. The value of art forms, such as haiku or sonnets, presumably has a similar history: initially, I assume, these conventional forms had no value in themselves. The interests and commitments to them that poets and poetry lovers had was not, therefore, a response to a value in these poetic forms that was already there. Rather, their value emerged *from* the interests and commitments of people who were attracted to them, or who agreed to the strictures imposed by these forms just for fun or challenge. As an activity or practice gains recognition and popularity, as traditions develop and groups organize around it, the opportunities for valuable activities involving it multiply: one can not only play basketball, one can coach it, teach it, write about it. Even being a fan can be a strand in the fabric that connects one to others, supplying a ready topic of conversation or just a knowing bond that links one to one's neighbors or one's community.[10]

Acknowledging the fact that value can emerge from brute attraction or interest interacting with drives to excellence, creativity, and sociability, encourages us to recognize a continuum of value along which an activity or object can lie. More precisely, the value of an activity or object in an individual life will vary depending on the relationship that the individual has to it and the role it plays in her life. The documentary film *Wordplay* demonstrates the remarkable range of ways in which crossword puzzles may contribute to a person's life, from those for whom it is a solitary daily ritual (and, as such, a mere harmless pleasure), to those who compete or create, to the incomparable Will Shortz, editor of the *New York Times* crossword puzzle, who graduated college with a degree in the self-devised major of enigmatology. Presumably, even lawn mower racing has, or can have, a place on this continuum.

Although Haidt and Arpaly offered their examples (of the horse-loving student and the goldfish-loving boy) as challenges to the idea that meaningfulness need be understood as essentially connected to objective value, I see their examples as offering hints about where objective value might be found and how it can emerge. By understanding their examples in this way, we can not only acknowledge the plausibility of their assessments, but explain what makes them so effective.

This discussion has also allowed me to bring out a point I made only abstractly in the lectures; namely, that the sense of objective value which, according to my view, is essential

---

[10] Go Heels!

to meaningfulness in life, is a far cry from the sort of pure, subject-independent metaphysical property that Plato or G. E. Moore had in mind. The kind of objectivity that seems necessary for meaning is a kind that implies that one can be mistaken about value. A person's liking something or thinking it to be valuable doesn't make it so (nor does her disliking something or thinking it not to be valuable make that so). Further, as it seems to me, a whole society's liking something or believing it to be valuable, doesn't make it so, all by itself. The discussions of basketball and poetic form suggest, however, that a person's or a group's liking something can *lead to* its becoming valuable. The attraction, or interest, especially if it is shared, can be an *opportunity* for value, an axis, initially neutral in itself, around which value forms.

This openness to the emergence of objective value out of brute human interest and attraction may lessen the resistance to the idea that some, like Haidt and Arpaly, initially have. At the same time, it may leave others either disappointed by what they see as a watering down of what is distinctive about my conception of meaningfulness or confused about what the point of it is, if it is to be understood so broadly.

The point, as I have said earlier, is not to defend any particular substantive view about what kinds of activities are worthwhile or what kinds of lives are meaningful, but rather to defend the categories and concepts that are needed to so much as formulate these views. In arguing that meaningfulness is a distinctive dimension of a good life, different from both happiness and moral goodness, and that the concept of meaningfulness is essentially tied to a commitment to objective distinctions in value, I have tried to show the importance of keeping the vocabulary of meaningfulness and value alive, and of not assimilating or reducing these terms to others that we are more comfortable with in both philosophy and popular culture. Only if we have these concepts, I believe, will we be able to understand some of our longings and sources of satisfaction, only then will we be able to properly assess some of our moral and other evaluative intuitions; and only then will we be able to ask questions and form hypotheses about what kinds of projects are worthwhile and what kinds of lives are meaningful.

Contributors

Susan Wolf is the Edna J. Koury Professor of Philosophy at the University of North Carolina at Chapel Hill. Her work ranges widely over topics in moral philosophy and the philosophy of mind. Before moving to Chapel Hill, Wolf taught at Harvard University, the University of Maryland, and the Johns Hopkins University. She is a member of the American Academy of Arts and Sciences and the American Philosophical Society, and is President of the Eastern Division of the American Philosophical Association for 2010–11. Her works include the classic articles "Moral Saints" (*The Journal of Philosophy* 1982) and "Sanity and the Metaphysics of Responsibility" (*Responsibility, Character, and the Emotions*, ed. F. D. Schoeman, Cambridge University Press, 1987), and a book on free will and moral responsibility, *Freedom Within Reason* (Oxford University Press, 1990).

Robert Adams, Distinguished Research Professor of Philosophy at the University of North Carolina at Chapel Hill, works in ethical theory, metaphysics, philosophy of religion, and the history of modern philosophy. He has taught philosophy at the University of Michigan, UCLA, Yale, and Oxford. Among the main topics of Adams's work has been the relation of religion to ethics, including theological responses to the problem of evil. His books include *The Virtue of Faith* (Oxford University Press, 1987), *Leibniz: Determinist, Theist, Idealist* (Oxford, 1994), and *A Theory of Virtue* (Oxford, 2006). Adams is a Fellow of the American Academy of Arts and Sciences and a Fellow of the British Academy.

Nomy Arpaly, Professor of Philosophy at Brown University, is interested in ethics, moral psychology, action theory, metaethics, and free will. She is the author of *Merit, Meaning and Human*

Bondage (Princeton University Press, 2006) and *Unprincipled Virtue: An Inquiry into Moral Agency* (Oxford University Press, 2002). Her journal articles include the following: "How It Is Not Like Diabetes: Mental Disorders and the Moral Psychologist" (*Nous* 2007); "Which Autonomy" (*Freedom and Determinism*, eds. J. K. Campbell, M. O'Rourke, and D. Shier, MIT Press, 2004); "Moral Responsibility, Applied Ethics and Complex Theories of Autonomy" (James Taylor, *Personal Autonomy*, Cambridge University Press, 2004); "Moral Worth" (*Journal of Philosophy*, 2002); "On Acting Rationally Against One's Best Judgment" (*Ethics*, 2000); and "Hamlet and the Utilitarians" (*Philosophical Studies*, 2000).

Jonathan Haidt is Professor of Psychology at the University of Virginia. His research examines the emotional basis of morality and the ways that morality varies across cultures. He has specialized in the emotions of moral disgust (which underlies much of the legal and social regulation of sexuality) and moral elevation (the entirely unstudied response to moral beauty). He is the author of *The Happiness Hypothesis: Finding Modern Truth in Ancient Wisdom* (Basic Books, 2006). In 2006–07, Haidt was the Laurance S. Rockefeller Visiting Professor for Distinguished Teaching at Princeton University. While there, he explored the role of moral motives in politics, the difficulties posed by moral diversity, and the techniques for reducing moralism and fostering civil discourse.

John Koethe is Distinguished Professor of Philosophy Emeritus at the University of Wisconsin-Milwaukee. He teaches courses on the philosophy of language, the philosophy of mind, epistemology, and Wittgenstein. His research focuses on the philosophy of language, Wittgenstein, and epistemology. He also publishes poetry and essays on literary theory. Among his publications are *Scepticism, Knowledge, and Forms of Reasoning* (Cornell University Press, 2005), *Poetry at One Remove: Essays* (University of Michigan

Press, 2000), *The Continuity of Wittgenstein's Thought* (Cornell, 1996), "Stanley and Williamson on Knowing How" (*The Journal of Philosophy* 2002), "And They Ain't Outside the Head Either," (*Synthese* 1992), "Contrary Impulses: the Tension between Theory and Poetry" (*Critical Inquiry* 1992), and several books of poetry, including *The Late Wisconsin Spring* (Princeton University Press, 1984), the prize-winning *Falling Water* (HarperCollins, 1997), *The Constructor* (HarperCollins, 1999). *North Point North: New and Selected Poems* (HarperCollins, 2002), *Sally's Hair* (HarperCollins, 2006), and *Ninety-fifth Street* (HarperCollins, 2009).

Stephen Macedo, formerly Director of the University Center for Human Values (2001–2009), is Laurance S. Rockefeller Professor of Politics and the University Center for Human Values. As founding director of Princeton's Program in Law and Public Affairs (1999–2001), he chaired the Princeton Project on Universal Jurisdiction, helped formulate the Princeton Principles on Universal Jurisdiction, and edited *Universal Jurisdiction: International Courts and the Prosecution of Serious Crimes Under International Law* (University of Pennsylvania, 2004). As vice president of the American Political Science Association he was first chair of its standing committee on Civic Education and Engagement and principal coauthor of *Democracy at Risk: How Political Choices Undermine Citizen Participation, and What We Can Do About It* (Brookings, 2005). His other books include *Diversity and Distrust: Civic Education in a Multicultural Democracy* (Harvard University Press, 2000); and *Liberal Virtues: Citizenship, Virtue, and Community in Liberal Constitutionalism* (Oxford University Press, 1990). He is coauthor and coeditor of *American Constitutional Interpretation*, with W. F. Murphy, J. E. Fleming, and S. A. Barber (Foundation Press, fourth edition 2008).

Index

CPSIA information can be obtained
at www.ICGtesting.com
Printed in the USA
JSHW052051170122
22061JS00001B/28

9 780691 154503